The memoirs of [Pete Lyon's] editing and film directing career in both Hollywood and Europe are a rich personal contribution to the understanding of moviemaking during the past fifty years. Often books of memoirs deal with only the glamorous. [This book] introduces the reader to the working areas of filmmaking that often remain out of sight. It is this effort to deal with the professional craftsman's attitude towards movies that will make the book informative reading for students of film.

-Frantisek Daniel
Former Dean, School of Cinema–Television,
University of Southern California

[The book] is very well written, informative, nostalgic, and personal...I was much impressed with [the] writing and the narrative skill.

-Bob Thomas
Associated Press Hollywood Correspondent

It has been our privilege at Hollywood High School to have reviewed ...*Twists of Fate*. This interesting narrative expressed in terms of his personal life would be a tremendous asset for those who may be interested in the motion picture field....It is not only interesting from the standpoint of a biography, but would be of tremendous value to schools whose curriculum included offerings in the entertainment and communications media.

-Hugh R. Foley
Principal, Hollywood High School

I have just had the pleasure of reading, and unfortunately finishing (I could have gone on for several more hours), *Twists of Fate*. First of all and most emphatically...I enjoyed it immensely ...a fine narrative style which manages to capture the sounds, tempo, light, and shadows of another era.

-Dr. Gene M. Gressley
Assistant to the President
University of Wyoming

I thoroughly enjoyed and learned from *Twists of Fate*... In thinking back over the impact of this book, I believe it is primarily a love story. A lifelong love affair between a dedicated professional, the movie industry and the people in it. Few of us can look back on our careers with such satisfaction and affection... For the young who are attracted to the entertainment business there is much to be learned here about the work of the writer, editor, director and producer. I've never seen this so clearly and simply discussed anywhere in print.

-William Voris
President Emeritus
American Graduate School of International Management

TWISTS OF FATE

An Oscar Winner's International Career

FRANCIS D. "PETE" LYON

EVANSTON PUBLISHING, INC.
EVANSTON, ILLINOIS 60201

EVANSTON PUBLISHING, INC.
1571 SHERMAN AVE., ANNEX C
EVANSTON, ILLINOIS 60201

Printed in the U.S.A.
All Rights Reserved.

10 9 8 7 6 5 4 3 2

ISBN: 1-879260-10-7

The only guide to a man is his conscience; the only shield to his memory is the rectitude and sincerity of his actions...With this shield, however the fates may play, we march always in the ranks of honor.

- Winston Churchill

CONTENTS

INTRODUCTION

The photographs and other framed memorabilia hanging on the walls of the comfortable study are intriguing: Walt Disney leaning out of the cab of a Civil War locomotive; a banquet menu signed by Winston Churchill, Sir Alexander Korda, and other famous Britons; a fan letter from director John Ford; a diploma from UCLA. On the coffee table is a handsome leather-encased scissors and letter opener set — a gift, the visitor learns, from Ingrid Bergman. "May I pick it up?" the movie-buff visitor asks. "Of course." As he is holding the scissors, his eyes fasten upon the most treasured item in the room: an Oscar, almost lost among the books on the shelves that line the wall behind the desk. "May I pick it up?" Again, "Of course."

It's a heady experience, holding an Oscar, even though it's not yours. But imagine hearing your name called on that climactic Hollywood night, the night of the Academy Awards, and being presented with an Oscar for your achievement. That was the thrill experienced by Francis D. Lyon when he was honored in 1948 with the best Film Editing award for *Body and Soul,* widely acknowledged to be one of the great prizefight movies.

"Pete" Lyon is now retired from the motion picture business, but his fascination with the art of film making has not lessened. He has frequently been asked such questions as, "How did you get into the movie business?" and "What does an editor (director, producer) do?" A few years ago, while browsing in a bookstore in Hollywood, Pete engaged in conversation with the owner, who when he learned of Pete's career, encouraged him to write a book about his experiences.

Twists of Fate is that book: a lively chronicle of the early days of movie making; the essentials of editing, directing, and producing; the contribution of film to the war effort; the special talents of such luminaries as Mack Sennett, Darryl Zanuck, David Selznick, Walt Disney, Charles Laughton, Laurence Olivier, Vivien Leigh, Ingrid Bergman, Leslie Howard, John Wayne, Montgomery Clift, H.G. Wells, Raymond Burr; and the Golden Age of television. If he knows any juicy tidbits about the many stars and directors and producers he has been associated with, he is not revealing them in this book. But stuffy the book is not. The reader becomes engrossed in the telling descriptions of movie legends at their most human and most vulnerable, *and* most temperamental.

This book is dedicated to young people, and to those not so young, who aspire to become the influential editors, directors, and producers of tomorrow, both in movies and in television. (Pete Lyon has assisted film students in the techniques of film making at the American Film Institute, filling a chair set up by the Academy of Motion Picture Arts and Sciences.) In addition to being an invaluable guide for students taking courses in film-making in secondary schools and colleges, *Twists of Fate* makes for fascinating reading for the general public as the author brings to life his fruitful career as film editor, director, and producer of films ranging from Mack Sennett comedies through World War II information films for the U.S. Army to post-war film classics and television series.

There is no self-aggrandizement in this book; nowhere is there evidence, as there is in so many books about Hollywood, of an author on an ego trip. Rather, a generous, self-effacing but determined nature permeates the book. Characteristically, Pete Lyon plans to give all the profits of this book to an educational foundation for scholarships.

Twists of Fate is a powerful educational tool as well as an important contribution to the literature of film making.

-Dr. Robert L. Page

Retired English teacher and book editor, Dr. Page shares with Pete Lyon a life-long fascination with motion pictures.

x

ACKNOWLEDGEMENTS

My gratitude to —

Milton Luboviski of the Larry Edmund Hollywood Book Store for his prodding to document what he called my unique experiences in films;

John Strauss, a prominent Hollywood publicist, for his interest and support;

William Hornbeck, who was patient with my early efforts at the Sennett Studios and a valued friend for most of my working life;

Dr. Robert Page, a former literary editor and teacher who received his Ph.D. in English at Yale University, and Charles R. Joyce, a fiction writer, for their favorable comments and suggestions;

David W. Ridgway, Executive Director of the Chemical Education Material Study, and Lincoln Bergman, both in the Lawrence Hall of Science at the University of California, Berkeley, for their thoughtful contributions;

Carol Sowell, for her help in wrapping up this project;

And my considerate, lovely wife, Ann, who has patiently lived through all these activities.

Others who gave me encouragement in writing this memoir include Bob Thomas, veteran Hollywood correspondent for the Associated Press, critic, and biographer; Dr. Gene Gressley, director of the University of Wyoming Library of Rare Books and Special Collections; Hugh R.

Foley, principal of Hollywood High School; Frantisek Daniel, former Dean of the Center for Advanced Film Studies at the American Film Institute and of the University of Southern California School of Cinema/TV; Bill Welch, Peter Johnson, and my film writer brother, Sumner J. Lyon.

Also, to Walter H. Bunker, a special note of appreciation for the serendipitous contributions received during the final stages of publication.

PROLOGUE

Herbert L. Lyon and his wife, Mary Davis Lyon, moved to North Dakota from Michigan in 1900 at the persuasion of Bert's brother, Fred Lyon, who had pioneered there as a young lawyer shortly after the Dakota Territory had been admitted to the Union as the states of North and South Dakota. Fred had been elected to the state legislature in the sparsely settled farming country of North Dakota.

In Michigan Bert and Mary had attended Ferris Institute, where they had taken courses in business, short-hand, and typing. With Fred's help, when they arrived in North Dakota they got jobs as court recorders, commuting to a few small-town courthouses as the need presented itself. The need arose often because they were well trained to document court procedures.

Soon Bert decided he wanted to get into a steady business. He convinced Fred that they and their wives should find a town with a future where they could fulfill their ambitions. They decided on Bowbells, a town of about 700 hardy people in the northwest corner of the state about 20 miles from the Canadian border. There they established the Lyon Land and Loan Company as a way of getting started.

Fred stayed until he thought Bert could make it on his own, then moved to California. Bert did quite well by branching out with insurance and real estate agencies and publishing the district newspaper.

In 1905, a son was born to Bert and Mary. He was named Francis after his mother's father, Francis Davis, who was native of Lansing, Michigan. Four years later another son, Sumner, arrived.

In 1910, Francis got to witness the passing of Halley's Comet, a very impressive phenomenon for a youngster of five years. Also impressive was the arrival of a traveling movie exhibitor who carried his wares from town to town. In towns where there were no regular movie houses, he set up his projection machine in any suitable hall he could rent inexpensively for a night or two. Francis found he could earn free admission by delivering handbills around town announcing the event. Perhaps this was the start of his interest in the movie business.

DEDICATION

This is the story of one of those many dedicated people in the motion picture industry who have been concerned primarily with the art of film-making. *Twists of Fate* is dedicated to the great number of students who are finding this expanding art form a gratifying means of expressing their talents.

ACTION!

The suspense is killing me! Those grossly misinformed people who say the results are known before that night! If some bright guy knows, I wish to hell he'd tell me now and get the agony over with. We're sweating through endless announcements and long acceptance speeches in too many categories. Is ours rated in importance by its position on the list? No, we really don't have a bad spot, but I wish they'd hurry on with it.

Half listening, half interested, but mainly squirming and nervous as a cat. Trying not to show it — trying to act like it's any other award night, any other Academy Award night. I glance toward Ann. She's probably more anxious than I, if possible, but she appears calm, and she smiles reassuringly. How does she do it? Bob is sitting next to me — he's no help. He twitches and shifts sides continually. Maybe he has more at stake — he's a lot younger — and nominated for an Oscar for his very first screen credit. That was a break in itself. Win or lose, he should have it made at his age.

Plenty of time to reflect upon the possibilities — five pictures nominated, all good jobs, tough competition. Are those editors fidgeting too? They have to be, but that's no consolation. What if we lose? We have to lose — can't think about winning — too much of a letdown if we don't win. That helps for a moment. Then, finally, we're on deck — we're up next!

Man, I'm perspiring pretty good now. What will I say if we win? On radio throughout the nation — will I embarrass myself? Ann? My friends? What am I worrying about? We're not going to win.

Anne Baxter, the presenter, is walking on stage. This is it. She reads the names and pictures nominated for the "Best Film Editing" award of the year 1947:

"Monica Collingwood, *The Bishop's Wife,* Goldwyn-RKO-Radio; Harmon Jones, *Gentlemen's Agreement,* Twentieth Century-Fox; George White, *Green Dolphin Street,* MGM; Francis D. Lyon and Robert Parrish, *Body and Soul,* Enterprise-United Artists; and Fergus McDonald, *Odd Man Out,* Rank-British." She opens the envelope.

"And — the winner is — winners are — Francis D. Lyon and Robert Parrish." What a jolt! The ambivalence of joy and fright. Here we go — we bounce up like a couple of school kids and stride down the long, long aisle to that huge stage before 6,000 watchers. That sweet, sweet Anne Baxter hands us the heavy statuettes. Scared to death, I stammer a few words of thanks and get off the stage as fast as possible. Backstage with the other recipients, I don't recall much except Darryl F. Zanuck, there via *Gentlemen's Agreement,* saying, "Well deserved."

Later, after reflecting on my acceptance remarks, I regretted not expressing appreciation especially to Wolfgang Reinhardt for his encouragement and to Howard Hawks for making me available.

Photo by Elmo Williams.

I believe it is appropriate to explain how Academy Award winners are selected because there is still some confusion among those outside the film industry about the procedure.

Since the Academy of Motion Picture Arts and Sciences first established the awards in 1927, when the film *Wings* received the "Best Production" Oscar, members of each of the several branches of the Academy have selected, by secret ballot, five nominees they believe to be the best examples of the work in that category for that award year. In 1992, for instance, Oscars were awarded in twenty-three categories.

After many screenings of the films that contain the nominated efforts, the members of the Academy vote, again by secret ballot, on what each decides is the best of the five nominees from all twenty-three categories.

The votes are tabulated by Price Waterhouse employees, who guard the results until the letters are opened by the presenters on award night. The winners are then announced to the worldwide audience.

Of course, because so much monetary value is riding on the results, especially for the "Best Picture," nominees may apply some pressure for votes. However, the Academy's Board of Governors has for years attempted to eliminate this effort with apparent success.

The final awards express the opinion of the majority of the nearly 5,000 Academy members and are highly valued by the recipients in all categories.

The Board of Governors is made up of two elected representatives from each of the Academy's creative categories, and each serves a three-year term. To gain membership, applicants must be sponsored by two members. They

Some of the founders of the academy standing l. to r. — Cedric Gibbons, J.A. Ball, Carey Wilson, George Cohen, Edwin Loeb, Fred Beetson, Frank Lloyd, Roy Pomeroy, John Stahl, Harry Rapf. Seated are Louis B. Mayer, Conrad Nagel, Mary Pickford, Douglas Fairbanks, Frank Woods, M.C. Levee, Joseph M. Schenck, Fred Niblo.

Francis D. Lyon, back row, sixth from left, served as a Board of Governors member of the Academy of Motion Picture Arts and Sciences, 1954-56.

are judged on the basis of a review of their talents in their respective crafts.

Possibly the best way to explain how my life happened to go through so many interesting changes, and to review many of the events that led up to the *important* issue of that night and my subsequent experiences in films, would be to answer the questions I have been asked so often through the years, starting with that most inquisitive of all:

"How did you happen to get into the movie business?"

That question — How did you get into this remarkable business anyway? — indicates a certain fascination with the fact that people who otherwise seem to be fairly normal are actually employed in the creation of entertainment, a field where it is generally assumed that far-out or unusual types of humanity are the main contributors. The question implies surprise that the Hollywood syndrome in action does contain some conservative variants. I suppose one can, to a certain extent, attribute those attitudes to the vast amount of publicity, good and bad, exciting and embarrassing, that our industry has received over the years.

I won an Academy Award, sure, but I've never been able to tell those talented young people who have come to me for guidance how *they* can make it. All I can say is, here's how it happened to me ...

In this account of some of my associations and activities in film-making, I hope the detailed and somewhat involved personal developments will prove to be of interest to those who may have experienced similar events, and perhaps offer some enlightenment to those who may wish to pursue comparable routes. I include some anecdotes about past and present film personalities whom I got to know well. That gives me a chance to do some name dropping and satisfy some public curiosity about such personalities, but more importantly, I hope this account sheds some light on those who have contributed so much to the history of a great enterprise.

Most of the disclosures here are relevant and contribute in some way to the conscious or unconscious decisions that have determined the course of one life in the movie business. This condition that we all experience, I call "twists of fate."

REEL 1

HOW DID YOU HAPPEN TO
GET INTO THE MOVIE BUSINESS?

Reel 1 of this epic begins in 1922, with a junior in Central High School in Minneapolis, Minnesota, pleading with his parents, by then retired, to move to Hollywood, California. I don't recall how I knew Hollywood had a high school, but I knew I wanted to get into the middle of the motion picture business, and Hollywood was where it was.

As a youngster, before moving to Minneapolis, I had been exposed to the crudely made films that traveling exhibitors set up in towns with no movie houses and also to the Saturday matinees of movie houses in larger towns. My brother, Sumner, and I were often given the ten cents admission fee by our parents to get us out of the house for a while.

The Mack Sennett comedies, like the Keystone Kops and other fascinating silent films of the time, must have planted a seed in my child's mind that sprouted a plan to somehow find a way to participate in that exciting entertainment business.

Fortunately it didn't take too much prompting to persuade my family to exchange the midwestern climate for the sunny skies of California. One reason was my father's brother, Fred, who was now a lawyer with the Internal Revenue Service in Los Angeles. Fred had been suggesting that we move to that area. We could stay with his family until we found a satisfactory place to live. Of course that place was in Hollywood, where we first settled on Gordon Street north of Sunset Boulevard near the busy corner of Gower and Sunset.

The Christie Brothers Studio, the Stern Brothers Studio, and other poverty row companies such as Columbia, Joe Rock, and Horsley were all located at or near this intersection. It wasn't unusual for me to pass through two or three companies shooting movies on Sunset at the same time as I walked along the pepper tree-lined street to Highland Avenue where Hollywood High is still located.

The Charles Chaplin studio was a short walk down the street from the school, and it was common to see Chaplin and his entourage stroll by at lunchtime toward Hollywood Boulevard. Frequently he would stop and chat with the high school girls eating their lunches as they sat on the low curb by the sidewalk. For some reason this attention disturbed the male student leaders. One noon, a group of athletes let Mr. Chaplin know quite pointedly their wishes for him to discontinue this practice. I believe he complied. The boys couldn't do much about the motorists, however, who slowly drove by the school at noon to ogle the young women as they lined the curbs, apparently unconscious or unconcerned about their exposed attitudes. At any rate, this feminine display was a notorious hazard for Sunset and Highland traffic.

I was seventeen years old, and Hollywood was a joy for me. Even my expectations were exceeded.

Hollywood Boulevard had a small-town atmosphere, scented with citrus blossoms from trees left from groves that had covered the area before movie people had discovered it. One could walk along the street and recognize faces that one could only have seen before on theater screens. It almost seemed like being among old friends one hadn't seen for a while.

On our way home, after baseball practice for instance, a few of us would sometimes walk from Highland to

*Looking south onto Hollywood from Hill – 1905. (Bruce Torrence
Historical Collection)*

*Hollywood Blvd. looking east – 1922. (Bruce Torrence Historical
Collection.)*

Hollywood High School – 1927. (Bruce Torrence Historical Collection)

Charlie Chaplin's studio – 1925. (Bruce Torrence Historical Collection)

the corner of Hollywood and Vine, where there was a hot dog stand on a vacant lot. Couldn't wait for dinner, I suppose.

Later I acquired a second-hand one-cylinder Cleveland motorcycle. During a slight rain I was riding across the streetcar tracks turning to go down Vine to Sunset. The wheels slipped and the cycle flipped on top of me in the middle of the intersection of Hollywood and Vine, much to my embarrassment. I sold the machine for ten dollars that afternoon.

Streetcars provided popular transportation on several routes to downtown Los Angeles. For instance, one ran along Hollywood Boulevard; another ran from Lankershim (now North Hollywood) over Cahuenga Pass from the San Fernando Valley to Highland past the Hollywood Bowl and the high school to Santa Monica Boulevard, where it ran downtown. It passed Vermont Avenue, where the Southern Branch of the University of California was located.

Highland Avenue carries fond memories because on it I was graduated from both high school (1923) and UCLA (1928, at the Hollywood Bowl). Subsequently, we lived on the west slope of Whitley Heights overlooking Highland. Many film stars of the time, including Rudolph Valentino, lived on Whitley Heights. The streetcars on Highland proved to be convenient transportation to college and my subsequent jobs.

After graduating from high school I was able to get summer jobs as a laborer in the film studios to help pay my tuition at the Southern Branch, where I enrolled in the fall of 1923. (In my junior year the Southern Branch became UCLA, and today that campus houses Los Angeles City College.) I felt I should not burden my parents with providing me financial help any more and, because tuition at the college was only $25 a semester, I believed I could handle the costs by myself.

In my first two years at college, I got by with income from my summer jobs, even with the fifty-cents-per-hour pay. However, the fraternity system was very popular at the beginning of my sophomore year, and I was finally asked to join a local group that I thought was best for me. The initiation fee was just within my budget. What I didn't foresee was the affiliation the same year with the Phi Delta Theta International Fraternity. To pay the $50 initiation fee required for another membership, I had to seek a loan. The members kindly arranged it, and I was in debt. To pay it back I decided to stay out of school for a year to catch up financially and possibly return the following year.

There were no film courses at the university then, so I majored in political science and prelegal courses to prepare for law school if my movie plans didn't work out.

Fortunately, in 1925 jobs on the studio labor gangs were available. My assignments were varied, from digging ditches and striking lumber (pulling nails out of used lumber for reuse in building sets) to moving furniture and props to and from sets, driving trucks, running errands, sweeping out the mill where sets were constructed, gathering greenery for set dressing, and anything else that was needed that other craftsmen didn't do. Today this variety of experience isn't allowed. Unions prohibit crossing the job line, with at least four unions having jurisdiction over this selection of activities.

Although no union was involved, I recall an incident in my labor days when I was surprised at the attitude of a laboring group toward my efforts. I was enjoying the physical job of digging a hole in the back lot of the studio for a water pool that a stunt man was to fall into during a scene. The foreman asked me to slow down because the other workers thought I was trying to show them up. When I was a youngster it had never occurred to me that one couldn't always perform to his best abilities if he wished to.

Trying to improve my income from the studio labor departments during my year out of school, I got a job selling Fords at a Hollywood agency on a commission basis. This amounted to about $25 a sale. I must admit that even after punching doorbells around the neighborhood, I didn't have much luck closing deals.

During my two years at the Branch, I had told a couple of students that I was envious of their part-time jobs at Famous Players-Lasky Studios Time Office in a branch of the accounting department. The studio was then located at Sunset and Vine Streets in the center of Hollywood. In due course one of the students remembered my desire for a job there, and at the first opening he suggested me to his boss. My friend found me at the Ford agency and, since I had just sold a car, I wasn't as enthusiastic as before. However, he persuaded me to at least talk to the boss since he had given me such a good recommendation.

It actually didn't take much persuasion by the boss to get me on his payroll at $27.50 per week (no overtime). He wanted me to go to the Craig Shipyards in Long Beach as paymaster for the construction crews for *Old Ironsides*. This was a big-budget merchant marine-pirate film of 1926, directed by James Cruze and starring Esther Ralston, Charles Farrell, George Bancroft, and Wallace Beery. The studio had a large hull of a ship towed from Boston through the Panama Canal to the shipyards, where it and other boats were renovated to resemble vessels of the era. The construction foreman, Harry Streit, was very considerate. Because I was working long hours, I slept on the ship for convenience.

After about three months of the day and night routine required to keep up with three shifts of shipbuilders who demanded their pay with overtime figured to the penny and on time, I was transferred to the United Studios (now the Paramount lot) to act as paymaster. Famous Players had bought this studio and was rebuilding to suit its expanding needs before making the move. Our office handled the timekeeping and payroll for about 2,000 construction men during a crash remodeling program.

The United Studios lot, previously the Brunton Studio, had been occupied by several independent producers including United Artists, First National Productions, and Joseph M. Schenk productions. During previous summer vacations, I had worked there as a laborer for 50 cents an hour. I recall working a few days assisting the property man on the set of *The Son of the Sheik,* which starred Rudolph Valentino and Vilma Banky. At various times I was able to watch in awe such stars as Norma and Constance Talmadge, Ronald Colman, Colleen Moore, Charlie Murray, Bessie Love, Harry Langdon, Anna Q. Nilsson, Lewis Stone, and Mary Astor, and directors like Henry King, Harry Edwards, Frank Capra (getting his break on a Harry Langdon film), Irving Cummings, and Alfred Green.

Mervyn LeRoy was there as a gag man. Comedy directors often had gifted writers with them to create funny ideas that had not been suggested in the script. They were called "gag men." Frank Capra was one before his promotion to director.

In 1924, I often sneaked on the set where Henry King was directing *Stella Dallas,* a Samuel Goldwyn-United Artists production starring Belle Bennett, Ronald Colman, Lois Moran, Douglas Fairbanks Jr., Vera Lewis, Jean

Hersholt, and Alice Joyce — a formidable cast, even in those days.

For a while I was busy as a laborer at the Warner Brothers Studio at Sunset and Bronson, doing odd jobs in various departments. I could watch Monte Blue, Marie Prevost, Lew Cody, Pauline Frederick, Creighton Hale, and Rin Tin Tin, among others. Directors included Monta Bell and William Beaudine.

Because I had finished only two years at college, I asked the time-office chief at Lasky (now called Paramount Studios), H.E. McCroskey, to assign me to the night crew so I could take some courses and eventually get my degree. Why I thought a degree was so important I don't know. But since the studio had moved by this time and things had settled down a bit, Mr. McCroskey, who had been a benefactor to many film aspirants, put me in charge of the night crew with the added responsibility of balancing the books each night before I could go home. My hours were from 5:00 P.M. to whenever we got the job done. Sometimes those were long nights because we had about 2,200 employees on the payroll, and we couldn't be more than one cent off balance.

The main purpose of my job was to help determine the daily dollar cost of the studio's operation. This task, of course, required tabulating all labor costs, including the salaries of executives and stars. The daily sum was charged to the project in work or to overhead.

All craftsmen on hourly rates, such as laborers, carpenters, electricians, painters, property men, grips, set dressers, transportation personnel, wrote the identification numbers of the film projects and the hours they worked on each on their payroll cards daily and handed them in at the time-office window as they checked out.

The cards were then processed by time-office personnel, who often used calculators to figure the charges to the projects and the amount due the workers for that day. Then the cards were copied by IBM punch machine operators onto cards that were processed through a tabulator that printed the information on a roll of paper showing all the day's costs of each project in work. The roll also included overhead and salaried employees, producers, writers, directors, actors, film editors, department heads, etc. This cost accounting enabled the executives to examine the daily costs of all projects in production.

My first exposure to the salaries paid to the big-name movie people was quite a revelation. I was amazed at the figures paid to such people as B.P. Schulberg (head of production), Clara Bow, Wallace Beery, William Wellman, Mary Brian, Gary Cooper (just starting), Sam Jaffe (studio manager), Jack Oakie, William Powell, Adolphe Menjou, Madeleine Carroll, Raymond Hatton, Richard Dix, Ray Griffith, Douglas MacLean, William De Mille, Clarence Badger, Frank Tuttle, and Louis Gasnier. I can't deny that the knowledge of the kind of money these folks were taking home had something to do with my decision to stay in the business.

Because living costs then were comparatively low, I was impressed by those in the creative fields who made $1,000 and more weekly. They included executives, producers, writers, directors, and actors. Clara Bow, for instance, was a rising star on contract for $1,500 a week. Salaries as high as $500 or $700 were paid to talented people who were working their way up the ladder.

My $27.50 per week allowed me to register for a full schedule at UCLA, which I kept for the two years and two summers until I graduated in the spring of 1928. By the time I returned to school, I had definitely decided upon a career in film-making. So, while I majored in political science, I branched out into several other departments in the belief that a wide range of subjects might be valuable in my future in the movies. These subjects included psychology, geography, public speaking, international relations, and languages when I needed grade points. For some reason I could get good grades from a beginning language course.

The excitement of being on the fringes of the motion picture business kept my adrenaline flowing, and I felt the struggle of working full-time and going to school full-time was worth it.

The night routine in the time office was sometimes altered by a visit from a star, writer, or producer who was working overtime and wanted to take a break by talking to someone. They knew there was always someone in the time office.

Clara Bow, like many stars, often stayed overnight in her dressing room during shooting when she had an early makeup call. She visited our time office occasionally when she felt lonely. Like many of the stars in those days, she was friendly and approachable.

Sometimes when a company was shooting at night I would take a break and visit the set for a few minutes. One night a crew was shooting a test of a beautiful young girl. Out of curiosity I asked who she was and was told her name was Loretta Young. She was sixteen years old, and it was the start of a great career. At my last Phi Delt formal some time later, one of the members brought Loretta as his date. Of course we were impressed, as I presume he intended. (Much later, I edited a picture she starred in called *The Men in Her Life.* She played a ballerina, with choreography by George Balanchine. She was always a pleasure to watch.)

At the time of my return to school, movies were booming. There was fairly steady employment, making it attractive for the ambitious aspirant to try to prove that he belonged. Consequently, I believed that I could make it. My substitute plans for three more years of struggling through law school evaporated. The temptation and the challenge of succeeding in films won out.

REEL 2

HOW DID YOU BECOME
A FILM EDITOR?

In 1929 there were very few organizations of any kind of workers in the creative fields of motion pictures, and no influential unions or guilds. I believe the present editors' union was formed in 1937. Now there are requirements for lengthy apprenticeships and assisting before one is eligible to accept an editing assignment, regardless of talent. There might be exceptions if there were no qualified film technicians available, a rare possibility these days.

But in those days, no such union requirements stood in the way of a young man's opportunity. After receiving my B.A. degree from UCLA in the Hollywood Bowl (our graduating class was too large to be accommodated on campus), I transferred to the day crew of the time office of Paramount. (UCLA moved to the new campus at Westwood in 1929.)

After a few months of timekeeping, I moved on to the property department as a bookkeeper and checker of incoming and outgoing material. After a short time in the property office, I was offered a job in the editing department. It helped that I knew the department head's secretary, who was the sister of Mr. McCroskey, my boss at the time office. I had a choice of being a projectionist or working in the cutting room office, where orders for reprints and the dailies were received from the film laboratory after the negatives were developed and printed.

Fortunately I realized that film editing was a worthwhile background for any film work I hoped to do eventually, so I accepted a job in the receiving room, at 62 ½ cents per hour, or $5 a day for eight hours' effort, $30 per week.

But I got overtime, so I soon ran my checks up to around $60 a week. I was a rich man until the boss got wise, and put me on a flat $35 per week salary.

When I had finished my chores in the receiving room, which included running the coding machine to put corresponding numbers on both action and sound films for the purpose of synchronizing them, I would often stay on to see if I could help those editors who were working at night to catch up with the shooting companies. In this way I learned quite a bit about assisting, and in about three months I was assigned as an assistant to Doris Drought, one of four or five female editors then at Paramount.

Sound had been introduced in the movies by then, but it was new to some of the editors. As a matter of fact, there was a Silent Cutting Department for making silent versions of the pictures. These would be sold to the many markets throughout the world that hadn't yet installed sound equipment. To get some experience in cutting, I put the "out" scenes (those not selected for the sound version of the film) together in silent form for the first film on which I was the assistant editor. Apparently I did passably well because Doris recommended me to Geoffrey Shurlock, who was in charge of these silents. I cut two or three for him and he was most complimentary. Geoffrey Shurlock later became famous as the code administrator for the Motion Picture Association of America.

Later I was assigned to Merrill White, who was in charge of sound cutting — that is, assembling the effects, music, and dialogue for mixing or dubbing. Since the Ernst Lubitsch musicals starring Jeanette MacDonald, Dennis King, Maurice Chevalier, John Boles, and their contemporaries were in vogue, I got great experience in procedures for sound and music cutting.

In a few months, I was back in the cutting room assisting another editor who had little experience with sound. She seemed frightened and confused with the extra film that contained the sound track. Her bewilderment turned out to be a great chance for me, because I found myself cutting *Her Wedding Night* starring Clara Bow, Charles Ruggles, Ralph Forbes, Betty Compson, and Skeets Gallagher. In fact, the editor acted as *my* assistant.

The basic tool used by the film editor was the moviola, an electrically driven means of projecting film to an aperture over a light, topped with a magnifying glass, which enlarged the picture four or five times. This allowed the viewer to observe, evaluate, and mark a scene for cutting or change. The film was moved forward or backward intermittently by sprockets, normally at the same speed at which it would be projected in the theater. Today's moviolas facilitate editing better than the first machines.

Bill Hornbeck at a vintage moviola. Note the rolls of sound track and picture on table ready for editing.

Both the picture and the sound can be run and projected on a small screen at any speed, in synchronization or separately, using 16mm or 35mm film or videotape.

There were very few sound moviolas available in those days, and an editor had to read lips and the striations on the silent track to know where to cut. I would have to run down the hall with a complete sequence to the only sound moviola on the floor to check the results. The script girls (two to a picture then — one for action and one for dialogue) had to type up exact dialogue for each take to facilitate editing.

I wasn't invited to the first-cut running of *Her Wedding Night* with the director, Frank Tuttle, but after the running I heard him congratulate the editor for an excellent job. Of course, that remark gave me the confidence I needed. And the picture received very good reviews.

There was no use fretting about not being asked to the first-cut running, and it really didn't bother me very much because I was gratified that this twist of fate had presented me the opportunity to prove to myself that I *could* do the job. It would possibly have taken many months for it to happen otherwise. Anyway, it was no secret to the department members what was going on in our cutting room.

For a time Paramount was making sound versions of some of its successful films in French and Spanish. American stars who were bilingual were often used. Adolphe Menjou, for instance, spoke very good French so he starred in one or two of these films. Cyril Gardner directed most of them, I believe.

Eddie Dmytryk, later an important director, was cutting for Gardner, and I was assigned as his assistant. Because I knew a little French (from school), he let me cut the French versions and he took on the Spanish ones. This work afforded me an excellent chance to get experience, and Eddie was very considerate at a time when I could use his help.

For clarification, the terms "film editor" and "cutter" are synonymous, as are the terms "edit" and "cut" and the terms "editing room" and "cutting room." In the silent film days, the term "cutter" was given to the person who used scissors to cut from one scene of a film to another at his discretion. It was an obvious description of his job. A "first cut" is the first assembly of cut film the editor or cutter has made to show to his director and producer.

The term "cutter" or "editor" is also used by other departments, such as those that handle music, sound, effects, and negative and cut film or tape as part of their assignments. The title "film editor" has become more acceptable, perhaps, because it is explicit and obviously more sophisticated than "cutter."

WHAT DOES A FILM EDITOR DO?

The work of a film editor is at best complicated, and often it's not comprehended even by those close to the production of films. One almost has to do it to understand it.

The bottom line, however, is this: the editorial department assumes physical control of the film when it comes from the laboratory where each day's shooting results are developed and printed overnight, until the approved final edited picture, negative, and dubbed sound track are delivered to the distributor.

At this final stage, a corrected, combined action and sound (or married print, as the English call it) is ready for showing in the theater. Tapes of dialogue, music, and sound effects, called three-stripe, are assembled on film for foreign and domestic dubbing where required. Continuity scripts, i.e., scripts that describe every cut, scene number, spoken word, progressively totaled length of each cut, and total length of the picture, are sent along with the film. Since the film is projected at 90 feet per minute, a picture's screening time can be calculated by knowing the overall length of the picture.

Those interested in the technical and mechanical operations of film editing might find the following description enlightening.

Step by step, the negative raw stock of the film in the camera is marked at the beginning of the scene to be photographed, by scene and take numbers corresponding to the script numbers. For instance, at the start of principal photography, say Scene 31, Take 1, happens to be a full shot establishing the geography of the set and action. Take 1 is the first attempt at recording the action staged by the director after he has been satisfied with his rehearsals. After a few attempts, or takes, to get satisfactory performances from the actors, perhaps he decides to settle on two takes to be printed.

The camera assistant circles those numbers on his camera report to the lab — say Takes 2 and 5 — to be printed in the laboratory from the exposed negative. The script supervisor makes notes on his or her report, also sent to the editor daily, describing the action and any deviations from the script that the director approves. Perhaps the director liked the last part of Take 2 and the first part of Take 5. Since he is going to cover the action with closer angles, the editor will be able to bridge the two takes by cutting from Take 5 when he chooses, to the close-up, then back to Take 2 for the selected action. The closer shots might be numbered 31A-1, 31B-1, etc.

Synchronization marks are placed at the head of each scene by a shot of a clapper-board containing the scene and take numbers, or by a camera light system that exposes a flare on the film and the identification numbers. The sound recorder also has his sync mark, either by the sound of the clapper-board or exposure mark, and the scene numbers corresponding to the camera's.

When the previous day's results are finished in the laboratory, the assistant editor assembles the film sound and picture, in synchronization and in continuity on 1,000-foot reels, for viewing by the director, producer, and editor. These bits of film are called rushes or dailies.

If all is in order, the assistant attends to the coding or numbering, foot by foot, on the edge of the film and corresponding sound track. That is, he starts at the beginning of each matching reel of track and picture that he has assembled for the dailies with an identification number, which the coding machine ink-stamps progressively every foot to the end of the reels. Thus the editor is able to synchronize the sound track and picture at any time during editing by matching the coded numbers. The assistant keeps books that catalogue the code numbers with scene numbers so that any trim or take can be easily identified during the editing process. After coding, the assistant breaks down (disassembles) the dailies and places the rolls, scene by scene, in continuity on the editor's work bench.

Although for economic reasons some television documentary and commercial films are shot on 16mm film, most entertainment pictures use 35mm picture negative, often with a taped sound track in 16mm.

Cutting, like painting, sculpture, and other arts, is a trial-and-error effort. During the first cut, the editor can make changes as he wishes, lengthen or shorten cuts, change angles, and make other major adjustments. He knows that timing, rhythm, flow of a scene, sequence of scenes, and transitions between scenes are important to the picture's entertainment value. The editor can sometimes correct or improve an actor's delivery of lines or a facial expression or body gesture by the manipulation of film.

For instance, he or she might have one or two of the "out" takes (those not selected by the director) printed up to see if a better reading of a line, or some required facial expression not evidenced in the selected takes, can be found. He might "steal" cuts from other shots not intended for use in a section he is working on if they present the desired effect. In other words, by using his imagination and ingenuity he decides how to get the most out of the film that is presented to him. He also does this by knowing where and when he should make cuts, how long they should be, where to overlay dialogue, and by using any other means that will most effectively interpret the screenwriter's and the director's efforts. It is in such decisions that the editor's artistic ability is made evident.

Of course, the director has the right to present his or her version of the editing to the producer, so the relationship of editor and director is important and can be made pleasant by a mutual aim at making the best motion picture possible. Cooperation between them, the producer, and, of course, the cinematographer during shooting, are especially beneficial to that end.

I will attempt to describe some of the mechanical processes of editing in more detail for those who are interested.

The editor places the picture and track in sync on his viewing machine by use of the corresponding code numbers. He runs the film to the place where he wishes to cut to the next angle, probably a closer one to emphasize a story point. He marks the spot with a soft pencil and puts the film in a hand splicer which has a blade that, when lowered, cuts the film on the frame line. The editor then decides, by running the next selected scene in the moviola, where to cut into it and places both ends of the film in the splicer where he attaches them with a sprocketed piece of adhesive tape over the butt ends of both outgoing and incoming scenes. This tape holds very well but it is easy to remove when changes are desired. Each joined scene is then wound onto 1,000-foot reels on the editor's bench. This cut-and-splice procedure is followed until the sequence is finished or the reel is full.

This procedure of editing, using moviolas of various vintages, was prevalent during my time as a film editor. Today, modern mechanical and electronic equipment is used for both film and videotape, streamlining methods and time to some degree. However, the same principles of good editing are achieved by whatever method and tools are used.

After the editor has assembled a few cut sequences to his satisfaction, he often arranges screenings during production so that the producer and director can evaluate his interpretations. From these runnings, the three film-makers can judge the need for retakes or added scenes or changes in cutting. The editing will continue until the director is satisfied that the best results have been achieved with his material.

After final editing has been approved by the producer, the editor assigns sound and music editors to prepare for dubbing — the mixing of music, sound effects, and dialogue together on one sound track. The effects editor assembles and synchronizes sounds as indicated by the film action. He makes out cue sheets for the mixers, indicating the footage where the effects are to be placed. The music editor measures the cues decided upon by the composer, producer, director, and editor for spots where the music will enhance the film's emotional or dramatic values. After the music is recorded, he places the tracks on a reel in sync with the indicated scenes and makes out cue sheets.

In the meantime, the film's editor arranges for any visual film effects, dissolves and fades, inserts such as close shots of newspaper headlines, letters, or any other objects that need underlining to strengthen story points. Main and end titles for required credits are often his responsibility to complete by the time of negative cutting.

That time comes soon after the lengthy dubbing or mixing sessions where the dialogue, effects, and music are blended together through the sound mixer's panel. This usually requires three able specialists who view the projected picture and perform accordingly by fading the sound tracks in and out on cue for the desired result. After all concerned are satisfied with the results, a preview of the work print is usually arranged at a theater that can project separate picture and taped track for audience reaction. A place like that is sometimes hard to find. The film editor will undoubtedly sweat out these viewings in fear that his splices might break, or the film get out of sync, or the audience might not like the film, or that dozens of other things will go wrong.

Previewing before an audience in a typical movie house is extremely valuable for determining how the results of the efforts from all concerned are accepted. The preview is the moment of truth that shows how the picture plays overall, how individual sequences and scenes work, how shots are timed. Some might be too long or short, and the audience usually indicates this. A laugh might occur at the wrong place, or might be cut short if the next line or reaction shot intrudes. This preview process is where the "timing" is tested. Experienced picture personnel can feel an audience's reaction as the film is projected.

It is often desirable to preview in theaters in various locations before different types of audiences to check on the reactions. They are not always consistent. But the preview provides very effective guidance for finalizing the end result. When the final editing is achieved, the work print is handed over to the negative cutters at the laboratory for matching.

These technicians select the negative scenes they have catalogued by the edge numbers printed on the raw stock by the film manufacturers (like Eastman). They then match the negative, cut by cut, with the work print that the editor has forwarded. The coded numbers placed on the positive for editing do not interfere with the negative numbers that are printed through to the positive because of quality differences. By the way, the negative is spliced together with quick-drying cement placed over scraped emulsion and sealed by electrically heated blades. When the negative cutters are finished, they give the picture to the laboratory for printing. The dubbed sound track, now on film, is usually on a full reel so they need only to sync both track and picture for the lab by splicing 13-foot "Academy" sync leaders on the heads of both. A composite answer print with the sound track on the side of the picture is then ready for normal theater projection.

The first answer print is viewed by the editor and a lab technician to check synchronization, light changes in printing, and quality. When the print is okayed, the editor gives an order for the final answer print to be made and mounted on 2,000-foot reels for delivery to the distributor. As a wrap-up, he might order scenes for the trailer (teaser or preview) for pre-exhibition showings, and prepare the storage of trims, out takes, dubbing units, work print, and other pieces of film not included in the final print.

The film is made, and the editor's work is done. If he is a freelance editor he is either on another assignment or looking for one.

These are the general procedures of the editor's job, though there are many variations, depending on whether an editor works at a major studio where functions are usually departmentalized, or for an independent company where the editor does more than the normal call of duty, or works for a relative. Editing of videotape involves somewhat different techniques but the principles of presentation are consistent.

Though my early years as a film editor were busy and demanding, not all was work. As a diversion in the late 1920s, the studios formed a basketball league, and I was picked to coach the Paramount team. Although I had been on the UCLA squad as a sophomore, I wasn't a very good player, but I guess there weren't any better athletes around the studios who had an interest in the job. To keep in shape one winter I played at the Hollywood YMCA with a good team that included John Lehners, later an All-American at the University of Southern California. During practice John dubbed me with the nickname "Pete," which has stuck with me all these years. Lehners graduated from USC law school, and for years was a business agent for the film editors' union and very influential in industry-labor relations. He also served as president of the important Motion Picture Council.

To make up a respectable Paramount team I enticed a few players from the Y team and the rest mainly from UCLA. Buddy Rogers and Solly Biano were the only two to try out from the studio. Buddy, from the University of Kansas, was an active film star, too busy to be much help in basketball. Solly, from the University of Illinois, had been a set-side violinist in the silent days, as a member of a three-piece group playing mood music for the actors. Later Solly became head of casting for Warner Brothers.

In 1929 several of us in the Paramount cutting department were laid off because of a production hiatus.

Francis D. Lyon, right, with the rest of the editing department at Mack Sennett Studios, May, 1932. William Hornbeck, editor-in-chief, is third from right.

One of the women editors suggested I check with William (Bill) Hornbeck, supervising film editor at Mack Sennett Studios, because she heard that he might need an editor, and she knew he didn't hire women editors. The reason might have been because Mr. Sennett had a reputation for being gruff and demanding of his employees. Perhaps he felt uncomfortable in dealing professionally with female technicians. There were several women editors in the studios then, as there are now.

To avoid making a trip over the Cahuenga Pass out to the Sennett Studios, I telephoned Bill. He said there were no openings but he took my phone number for future reference. The future arrived about six weeks later, and Bill hired me to cut a comedy for him for $75 a week — a nice step up from the $35 I received at Paramount.

Mack Sennett comedies were famous for fast action and broad situations. They were probably the most successful short films in the late 1920s. At that time the company trademark was a white spotted bulldog framed in the door of a large doghouse. At the opening of each picture, he perked up his ears, cocked his head, and barked — a takeoff on the lion in the famous MGM trademark.

The man who headed this film factory was not unlike the bulldog he selected to designate his product. Mack Sennett was in fact a bull of a man. His large head, topped by a heavy white mane, was set on a thick neck. His broad shoulders, scowling features, and deep throaty voice all contributed to an impression of power and dominance that provoked fear and awe in many who came in contact with him — especially a number of his employees. He was unable to hide his feelings, good or bad. At least he commanded attention.

Talking with ex-employees who visited the editing department, I soon learned that they indeed did not want an encounter with Mr. Sennett. When they saw him approaching, they took off quickly.

I made up my mind not to be cowed by Mr. Sennett or by anyone associated with my work in films. I concluded that I had nothing to lose and much to gain by being forthright in offering opinions that I believed could contribute to a solution for any problem at hand. This attitude apparently worked well because Mr. Sennett was receptive to my comments, and I was comfortable in my relations with him and others in the studio.

Sennett had an unusually loud and raucous laugh, which exploded often as he viewed his films in the studio projection room. It was his custom to preview first cuts before neighborhood people who were invited to the studio nearly every Friday night to offer reactions. I often wondered at the value of these runnings because, by his own laughter, Sennett usually cued the audience when to laugh. The other viewers were seldom ahead of him, and sometimes not even with him.

Among the projects in work when I caught on at Sennett's were the comedy series of Andy Clyde, Bill Bevan, W.C. Fields, and the All-Star comedies (with Marjorie Beebe, Agnes Moorehead, Harry Gribbon, Fifi D'Orsay, Eddie Gribbon, etc.). It was a busy place, affording me ample opportunity to observe many facets of film-making that were new to me. All I needed to do was to hang on to the job — a real challenge for a young punk with more nerve than sense. Two other editors working for Bill were Bob Crandall and Malcolm Knight, both conscientious gentlemen.

As it developed, I received a unique schooling at the Mack Sennett Studios. My first assignment was to cut a two-reeler directed by one of the staff writers, who had been given his first chance at directing. It turned out to be his last. His approach to camera coverage was foreign to anything I had experienced and, as a neophyte in comedy cutting, I thought this might be *my* last motion picture venture. Thanks to Bill Hornbeck's patience and guidance, I eventually got the film together and was assigned to another one. This second film was also directed by a first-timer, but this time it was Sennett's efficient, long-time assistant director, Babe Stafford.

In Stafford's picture, the star was Andy Clyde, a very popular actor at the time and a really nice guy. The story was something about Andy finding himself in bed with a big bear and the usual wild chase. Babe knew the mechanics of directing well and did a good job. His film went together quite easily, but as often happened, Sennett got antsy to see the cut picture before we were ready. He set a preview for Friday night after the Wednesday that I received the last day's rushes. That gave me three days (and nights) to get the picture into some kind of shape. I really felt concerned for two people — Babe and me.

Come that Friday night, I was still frantically throwing the film together. During this panic to meet the deadline, Babe Stafford nervously paced back and forth by my cutting room door, anxiously checking to see if I was going to make it. In this kind of comedy, a break between reels would be disastrous — especially to the future of the new director and the new editor. Somehow I finished just in time to get the second reel spliced and onto the projector as the first reel ended. Didn't miss a beat.

As the film showed, we could hear Sennett's laughter, more frequent and louder than usual, with hearty support from the audience. When the lights went on, the audience applauded enthusiastically and Sennett was still laughing. The two characters on trial that evening were relieved and pleased.

From then on, work at the Sennett studios was a comparative breeze for me. I got along fine with the "Old Man" and learned a lot from him about timing and delivery, important elements in films, especially in comedies. He seemed to like the fact that I was not in awe of him and that I spoke up when I thought I could contribute. He was honestly civil to me, and before long I even got a small raise.

I was able to buy a Ford at $75 down and $75 a month. Until then I had been driving Eddie Dmytryk's Ford while he was in New York cutting a Paramount feature.

The cutting routine at Sennett's was one of long hours with a fairly well-defined pattern of operation. It was a schedule I wouldn't welcome today, but then I was young, single, and ambitious. The Old Man didn't often show up in the morning. He slept late or played golf, then worked with the writers until evening. Some of those writing sessions were a sight to behold, with Sennett riding herd over a frustrated gang trying to comprehend the gags and situations he envisioned. He had a great imagination but lacked somewhat an ability to communicate ideas.

We ran cut film nearly every night around 8:30 P.M. Sennett would usually take some lady of that evening to dinner and often didn't show up until way after screening time. We got accustomed to his lateness so we would do some other work or listen to Bill Hornbeck's anecdotes while we waited. Bill had started with Sennett at the Edendale Studio around the beginning of World War I, so he had much to relate about the prominent old-timers and their experiences, especially with the boss. Most of his stories were funnier than some of the comedies we were releasing. Hornbeck told his stories well and often. Many have been documented and make good reading.

When the Old Man finally did arrive for the screening, he usually brought his gal of the evening. The editor would sit between the boss and the girl on the theory that he could get Sennett's suggestions for cutting changes as the film was being projected and make the changes the next day, so he could run the picture again the next night. The theory was reasonable but didn't always work out.

Mr. Sennett and his date usually had had a good dinner, with ample libation before, during, and after. He would be in a good humor, particularly if he anticipated further success with his lady after business hours.

Sennett, a tobacco chewer, placed a sand box by his seat on the aisle during screenings. The one sitting next to him had to mind the position of his own feet because the Old Man's relaxing dinner sometimes affected his aim, which wasn't too good to begin with. I learned this hazard of the job early and hastily made the necessary adjustments.

When the film started, the Old Man would start laughing in anticipation as soon as the bulldog appeared. Then he'd start again with the first gag and keep up his roar intermittently for about five minutes. About then his head would bow, and pretty soon some hefty snoring would start. The startled woman with him would look across at him, then at me, in amazement. Usually she would shrug her shoulders and lean back to enjoy the picture unless she was his steady of the moment, in which case she had seen it before.

When the picture was over and the lights came on, Sennett would awaken with a start, laugh out loud, and remind me to make those changes before tomorrow night. Then out he and his date would go. Usually I would note some changes I wished to make and get ready for a repeat performance the next night. So the evening wasn't a complete waste of time, for me anyway, though I sometimes wondered if it wasn't a waste for him.

The Old Man could get quite arbitrary about cuts he wanted and sometimes insisted upon unrealistic changes. Instead of fighting him too much, we would often agree to try them. If there was no way to comply without ruining the picture, we would run the film again, without touching the part he wanted to change. Invariably he assured us the change worked well, and we agreed that we should have done it that way in the first place. Most film editors have experienced this procedure many times. Film can be a fooler.

W.C. Fields was a good friend of Sennett's and a good moneymaker for the studio. I edited one or two of his comedies with great pleasure. Fields was an artist who projected great magnetism on the screen. His Sennett films, *The Dentist, The Fatal Glass of Beer, The Barber Shop,* and *The Pharmacist,* are now classics.

Around the studio, Fields was quiet and pretty much a loner. There were some memorable exceptions when it appeared the juice became a bit powerful or someone crossed him at the wrong time. Wearing his funny top hat and carrying the perennial highball glass, he often came into the projection room to see his dailies. He would sit down without a word and would leave the same way. He was all business on the set and tolerated no nonsense.

During the early and mid 1930s, I was impressed with the potential of the comedy musical short subject. When Bing Crosby, a terrific success as the lead singer with the Rhythm Boys at the Coconut Grove in the Ambassador Hotel in Los Angeles, suddenly became available, I suggested to Mr. Sennett that he attempt to get Crosby out to the studio for a film test. At first Sennett resisted my interest, and it took me days of persuasion to get him to acquiesce.

Bing and Dixie arrived in an old, beat-up topless roadster (a Nash, I think), looking as though they didn't have a sou.

The results of the test more than vindicated my efforts to sell the Old Man on Bing's potential. His great personality came across well on the screen. Sennett signed him to a mutually favorable contract. Our faith was substantiated in the years to come. Crosby never knew of my small interest in his career, but I was rewarded in my assignments as editor of his films, such as *I Surrender, Dear* and *In the Blue of the Night*.

Around this time two twists of fate occurred.

One was that my success with the Crosby deal prompted me to try for a substantial raise for my efforts. Bill Hornbeck was supportive, which, of course, gave me hope.

I met with the studio manager and told him my wish for more money. He reluctantly offered a $10 boost to $85 a week. I screwed up my courage to strike while hot and calmly told him I wanted to leave for a better chance at the Fox studio where I knew they paid $150. I said I would give him two weeks' notice, which meant I would leave about the time I finished my present assignment.

He squirmed a bit, and I hoped he didn't notice my anxiety while he mulled that over. Then he told me that Mr. Sennett planned to have me direct the next Crosby series, which was expected to be renewed by Paramount in the near future. I almost gasped aloud, but kept my poise somehow until he asked if I would stay for $125 a week. I quickly said yes and left his office before he could change his mind.

The second twist of fate was related to my personal life. I had always intended to delay any involvement relating to marriage until I had it made financially. My work at the studios had curtailed activities at college, and my social opportunities were in short supply.

Sometime after graduating from UCLA and while working at the Sennett studio, I visited my fraternity house to see how the members were doing. They happened to be having an informal gathering at the Kappa Kappa Gamma sorority house next door that Sunday afternoon. The Phi Delts had a good piano player who could supply music for dancing. So they asked me to join them.

I met Ann Coursen at that gathering. She was a pledge, having attended the Marlborough School for Girls in Los Angeles and Mills College in Oakland, California.

We dated for some social events, usually related to her connections. Often we went to the Coconut Grove at the Ambassador Hotel, where Bing Crosby, Harry Baris, and Al Rinker, the Rhythm Boys, performed.

My attitude about a later marriage contract gradually faded in the realization that I had a jewel in tow. I had better come down to reason before she recognized that I was chasing her until she caught me.

At any rate, we agreed to announce our engagement. The catch for me was her insistence that, as a matter of custom, I must ask her father for permission. She would set the time. I was more nervous about that confrontation than about the one when I asked for a raise.

Our meeting started with some irrelevant conversation until Mr. Coursen kindly broke the ice by saying he knew about our intentions. Coming to the point, he asked how much money I made. I said $125. In a tone that indicated this might be acceptable, he asked, "A month?" When I said, "No, a week," I thought he showed some incredulity. But, thank God, the deal was consummated. After a two-year engagement we were married on March 30, 1935.

The Crosby musicals were very successful at the box office, and Paramount, the distributor, seemed pleased with the product. But not with the costs. It seemed that Mr. Sennett had a habit of charging the costs of some of his extracurricular activities against his pictures, which ran all his films quite a bit over the budget that the producing and releasing companies had agreed upon. His expenses became a point of controversy, and the confrontation put the Sennett company's future in jeopardy.

As an aside, one day while I was working in my cutting room Paul Guerin, the studio's chief engineer, came in. He told me that due to the Depression, land in the San Fernando Valley was very cheap. He had bought as much as he could afford, and he knew of a parcel of ten acres not far from Studio City that he thought I should look at. I asked him why I should be interested in buying property anywhere during these times, especially in this valley. Then he said he knew the owner, who was desperately in need of cash and would sell it for $100 an acre. Paul said it was an incredibly low price, and he felt the valley had a great future when the economy improved, and that I should take advantage of this opportunity.

Although I probably had about that much money in the bank and perhaps Paul was right about the future, I didn't want to risk the money on such an investment, no matter how attractive, under my uncertain working situation. Considering what followed, perhaps this twist of fate wasn't as disastrous as it could have been.

One of the twists of fate in my career (like so many things that happen in Hollywood) was my assignment in 1933 to direct the next Bing Crosby series as soon as the Paramount releasing contract was renewed. But the contract was not renewed because of Sennett's money problems, and it was the end of the Mack Sennett era.

The studio at Studio City was taken over by receivership and set up as a rental facility. (Later on it became Republic Studios.) Bill Hornbeck and I were about the last Sennett employees on the receiver's payroll. Our assignment was to wrap up the editing department — that is, to prepare for storage the film library and any negative film of released pictures that was left.

Mr. Sennett was allowed to keep his office on the lot for a while. I stopped in one day to thank him for the opportunity to work for him and to say I had learned a lot during the experience. He was indeed a lonely man sitting at his desk, but seemed pleased with my visit. That was the last time I saw him.

No one was more crushed about the inactivity at the Sennett lot than Mack Sennett himself. He couldn't believe that there was no release available for his product. He continually spoke of producing a long-time favorite project of his, *Molly O.* But no one seemed interested and he died almost penniless, still making plans to get into production again. It was rumored that Bing Crosby paid his rent at the Garden Apartments on Hollywood Boulevard for some time before Sennett died.

Del Lord, a former Keystone Kop who had directed many comedies at Sennett's, was signed to direct a series with Walter Catlett and Eugene Pallette for Paramount release. I had cut some of his Sennett shows and he got me the editing job. These films were produced by Phil Ryan at the old Thomas Ince Studios in Culver City.

I was surprised during that experience by a call late one night from Ryan demanding that I come to the studio. He wanted to talk to me. I hurriedly dressed and arrived at his office some minutes later. When I entered he was at his desk, which had a revolver lying on it. I was startled, but tried not to show it. Actually Ryan didn't refer to the gun, but he seemed a bit uncertain about why he had called me. He rattled on about the progress of the projects, Del's direction, and my need to speed up the progress. I don't know what he meant because I was up to date with the editing and Del was pleased with the results. I left after concurring with his admonition.

When I told Del about this incident, he said to forget it, that Ryan was like that when he was drinking. He also said that Ryan had a thing for riding fire engines that were on call. Possibly he got permission for these escapades by declaring he was getting some atmosphere for a film he was planning. It takes all kinds, they say.

This job lasted a few months until that series was completed. Again looking for a job, I got a Charlie Chase comedy to cut at the Hal Roach Studio in Culver City. It was a one-shot deal.

The real Depression was now with us. Many businesses were in trouble, including the movies. Jobs were hard to come by. Few films were in production. Many experienced technicians dropped to lower-paying work if they could find it. The Hollywood Savings and Loan Bank had failed, leaving many movie people hurting for funds.

Even my good friend and benefactor, Bill Hornbeck, was having a tough time finding work during this period. I had an idea that I suggested to him because I felt he needed a change from Hollywood. He was single and wasn't hurting for money, so I convinced him to take a freighter from Los Angeles harbor through the Panama Canal to England. He knew Harold Young, who had been a film editor at Warner Brothers Studio when Alexander Korda had directed a film there a few years earlier. Korda later hired Harold as supervising editor at this important London Film Company. I thought Bill might catch on with the growing English industry. At any rate, it would be worth the effort for him if nothing came of it because he liked the freighter idea.

The twist of fate for him was that Harold Young had just been assigned by Korda to direct Leslie Howard and Merle Oberon in *The Scarlet Pimpernel.* Bill was immediately hired to replace him, and in a short time he achieved well-deserved success with the company.

Although I thought I had saved enough money to keep us going, it soon ran out and, to put it mildly, it was frightening. Ann got a part-time social work job with the state that didn't pay much, while I struggled on, at times assisting any lucky editor who needed extra help.

This frustration went on for months. Then at long last we were rescued from the United States' Great Depression by a most fortunate twist of fate.

TWISTS OF FATE ACROSS THE SEA

EUROPE

This reel of my script begins in 1935, the low point of the Great Depression.

For a newlywed who had been out of work for months with no job in sight to get a cable from London Film Productions, Ltd., one morning at 8:00 A.M. requesting his presence in England as soon as possible for a six-month contract was the thrill of a lifetime. The Korda studio's growing schedule of films created a need for experienced film editors, so Bill Hornbeck arranged for the company to send for me post-haste.

A happy couple arranged departure by train to New York that same evening at 8:00 P.M., then traveled by the Holland American Steamship *Veedam* to land at Plymouth Harbor in England two weeks later.

It was undoubtedly the exuberance of youth, but I believe I still would experience the same excitement of landing on foreign soil for the first time. Even knowing through reading and films about the Europe's monetary, speech, traffic, and architectural differences, seeing them for oneself still creates an almost unrealistic but exhilarating impression. Happily this attitude persists if one feels the character of a new land and understands that every contact with a strange people can be a novel experience. It helps if they are approached in a reasonable friendly manner, of course.

The period from 1935 to 1939 was an interesting time to be an American motion picture technician employed in London. These were four very exciting years of

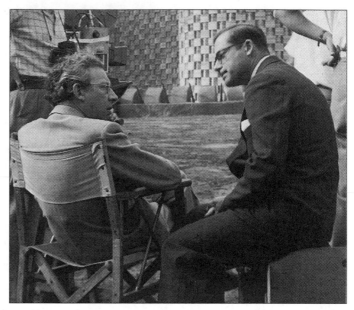

Sir Alexander Korda and Bill Hornbeck in conference.

history for Great Britain and for its expanding film industry. This phase of my life brought me into contact with
some of the great personalities in the film business and in
the country's politics.

Bill Hornbeck influenced my career because of his
keen judgment and exceptional capabilities. I still consider
him to have been the outstanding film editor in our business. It was a fortunate twist of fate to have met him at the
Sennett Studio in 1930.

Upon our arrival in London, Bill got Ann and me
settled at the modern Mount Royal Hotel, then took me to
the studio to meet the Hon. Anthony Asquith, a successful
young director and son of Great Britain's Prime Minister
during World War I, Lord Oxford and Asquith.

After talking for about five minutes with "Puffin," as
Anthony was affectionately known by his friends, we left
the set. Bill laughed when I had to ask him what in hell

Asquith had said to me because I honestly didn't grasp the meaning of one complete sentence. Bill had anticipated, with amusement, my surprise and confusion over many of the English expressions and customs.

Tony, as I later came to call Asquith, was a graduate of Balliol College at Oxford and had the proper Oxonian accent, which is difficult for the untrained ear to understand. But before long I was able to dispense with an interpreter and, through our film association, Tony and I became very good friends.

My first assignment for London Films, then located at Worton Hall Studios in Hounslow, a suburb of London, was to edit a film called *I Stand Condemned* in the United States. It was produced by the head of London Films, Alexander Korda, directed by Anthony Asquith, and starred Laurence Olivier, Harry Baur, and Penelope Dudley-Ward.

The film was one of the first for Olivier, later to become Lord Olivier, who was already one of the premier stage actors in England. It was called *Moscow Nights* in Europe.

During a running of the dailies I noticed in a close-up that Olivier was attempting to show tension in a courtroom scene with a continual tic of an eyelid. The shot was important to the story but I couldn't find enough of it without the tic to use in cutting the sequence. The constant tic was disturbing and it had the opposite effect that Larry felt he was creating. He didn't need tricks in his acting, especially for film. When I brought the situation to Korda's attention he agreed and so did Tony. But Tony couldn't convince Larry to retake the close-up.

So I asked Olivier to come to the projection room and see the rushes for himself. To his credit, the running changed his attitude completely, and he pleaded with me to support his request for a retake. I believe he learned something from a film viewpoint in that one experience that helped him in his later film work. I found Larry to be a fine gentleman, very cooperative, and always a great actor.

Penelope Dudley-Ward, a promising actress at the time, was later married to the Oscar-winning English director of *Oliver!*, Sir Carol Reed.

The French actor Harry Baur had an important part in *I Stand Condemned*. He had a problem with English, so we had to replace every word he said in the film with a matching English actor's voice. It took me three long days to do it by looping, a technique then new to the business, and several days of replacing the dialogue tracks.

Looping is a editing process of replacing only the sound of lines that are unacceptable as recorded during production because of an undesirable reading, accent or offstage sound interference. It is cheaper and more controllable to have actors reread lines after shooting, on a sound stage where the director and or film editor can make satisfactory selection, than to shoot that portion of film again.

In the looping process, the editing department cuts out the film of each line to be replaced. It is spliced as a loop to be projected over and over so that all concerned can determine the proper reading and synchronization of lip movements. When the new lines are recorded and approved as satisfactorily fitting the picture, the next loop line is projected and the process continues until all objectionable lines are replaced.

Most often, an actor reads his own lines in looping. But in *I Stand Condemned,* another actor read all of Baur's lines, copying the tempo and readings to fit the action with perfect synchronization. In the finished film, I doubt that anyone except Mr. Baur and his intimates detected that his voice was not his own.

During my association with Tony Asquith, Ann and I were often invited to his home where he lived with his famous mother, the Countess of Oxford and Asquith, a most wonderful woman who was very well known in England's politics and philanthropic activities. She was a chain smoker who chatted incessantly, and was extremely entertaining and interesting to listen to.

Speaking rapidly and enthusiastically seemed to be a family trait. Lady Oxford's daughter, Princess Elizabeth Bibesco, Tony's sister who was married to the former Ambassador of Romania to the United States, and the Princess's daughter, Priscilla, were also at the Bedford Square home one evening when Ann and I were invited for dinner. The chattering at cocktails with all four pacing the library floor and speaking at the same time was something to hear. After enduring the cacophony for a few minutes, I jumped up and abruptly asked them to please take turns talking because I knew each had important and interesting things to say, but we Americans found it difficult to be attentive to more than two English voices simultaneously. They laughed and took the hint.

I don't remember when we enjoyed an evening more than that one with such a very bright and colorful family. Lady Oxford obviously liked Ann and kindly invited her to many functions during our stay in England. Sometimes we American colonists are accepted, it seems.

Elizabeth had spent some time in Washington, D.C., with her husband and, of course, knew many of our political and social leaders. She was one of the most intelligent women I have ever known. Her knowledge of our country and its political complications was far greater than most Americans ever achieve.

Margot, as Lady Oxford preferred us to call her, was an amazing hostess and often had English political leaders in her home when we were there. We appreciated this unusual opportunity to meet and converse with these people of varied experiences and viewpoints. Some had served with Lord Asquith and most were in the opposite party to the then Prime Minister Baldwin. Since I had been a political science major at UCLA, and had studied comparative governments and once considered the foreign service, you can well imagine my great interest in these meetings.

Early during our stay, the popular King George V died. One has to experience personally the pageantry and emotion the English display on ceremonial occasions to understand the importance they place on the royal family and what it represents to the history of Great Britain. In due course, after a most impressive funeral procession and burial of George V, the title passed to the Prince of Wales, later Duke of Windsor, as King Edward VIII. Our file of fond memories of that era in Great Britain is vividly filled with Edward's abdication of the throne and the events leading up to it — Baldwin's radio speech to the nation about the government's attitude toward Edward's proposed marriage to Mrs. Simpson; Edward's dramatic abdication speech; the crowning of his brother, King George VI; the subsequent opening of Parliament by the King and Queen, to which we were invited as guests of Margot Asquith.

It seemed that with all the distractions of the times, one would find it difficult to concentrate on our reason for being in England — the film industry. However, so much

Funeral procession of King George V, January 28, 1936.

was developing so rapidly in my work that there was really no chance of losing my ambition to be a part of its progress.

Other books present in detail the history of the film business in England, such as *Twenty Years of British Films — 1925-1945* by the Falcon Press, Ltd., and *Where We Came In* by Charles Oakley. I make no attempt to register all the people or events that were involved during those years or to review the chronological history of England during that time. My purpose is solely to indicate how two visiting Americans, thanks to their motion picture affiliation, became involved in some unusual and exciting events that made a most rewarding contribution to their lives.

London Film Productions, Ltd., was undoubtedly the most important of the producing companies in England in the late 1930s because it was well financed and had a most ambitious program. The head of production and the guiding hand in its growth was Alexander Korda, one of three Hungarian brothers then active in films.

Zoltan was a director and Vincent an art director of great talent. Alex also directed and perhaps got his first big acclaim as producer and director of *The Private Life of King Henry VIII,* starring Charles Laughton, Merle Oberon, Binnie Barnes, and Wendy Barrie. It established Laughton as an important actor and called attention to Britain as a new production area.

Soon to follow were *The Private Life of Don Juan,* starring Douglas Fairbanks Sr., Merle Oberon, and Benita Hume; *Sanders of the River,* directed in Africa by Zoltan Korda and starring Paul Robeson, Leslie Banks, and Nina McKinney; and the most successful, *The Scarlet Pimpernel,* directed by Harold Young and starring Leslie Howard and Merle Oberon, who later became Mrs. Alexander Korda.

It was due to the success of some of these early film efforts that Alex was able to get continuing financial support, but the international acclaim that *The Scarlet Pimpernel* achieved in 1935 opened up an almost unlimited source of money for him to plan a multiple picture program and a huge new studio facility at Denham, Bucks. In the main, financing was supplied by the tremendous Prudential Assurance Company of England. The funding appeared to be substantial because Alex soon announced several big projects and the acquisition of many stars and creators from Hollywood and other film production areas.

Most of Korda's associates called him "Alex" to distinguish him from his brothers. When Sir Winston Churchill was Prime Minister and Alex was knighted, he then was addressed as Sir Alexander. He was an imposing man, tall, dapper, always well groomed. He was a businesslike, no-nonsense executive, but certainly approachable and considerate. He attracted the best around him.

When we arrived in London, construction of the Denham Studios was already under way and the big-budgeted H.G. Wells story, *Things to Come,* starring Raymond Massey, Ralph Richardson, and Margaretta Scott, was nearing the end of shooting at Hounslow. The director was William Cameron Menzies, previously a famous American production designer. The film had been nearly two years in production.

A film from another H.G. Wells book, *The Man Who Could Work Miracles,* was being directed by Lothar Mendes and produced by Erich Pommer, and starred Roland Young, Ralph Richardson, and Joan Gardner (later Mrs. Zoltan Korda). Some other projects in various stages of development were *I, Claudius* and *Cyrano,* both to star Charles Laughton; *The History of the Flying Machine,* which some of the early aviation experts were researching; René Clair's *The Ghost Goes West,* starring Robert Donat and Eugene Pallette; James Hilton's *Knight without Armour,* starring Robert Donat and Marlene Dietrich; *Elephant Boy,* a Robert Flaherty picture shooting in India, starring Sabu; *Rembrandt,* starring Charles Laughton, Gertrude Lawrence, and Elsa Lanchester; *The Life of Marlborough,* which the then out-of-politics Winston Churchill was writing for Alex. There were others in a long list of important film materials, some of which were produced and many dropped.

Cans of dailies of *Moscow Nights* had piled up because the picture had been shooting for three weeks before I arrived on the job. This stack of work prompted my desire to catch up with shooting and I dived in with my Sennett-trained drive, not yet in tune with the more reasonable working pace of the English. After the first few days of silently sticking with me in the cutting room while the others took their tea break, Russell Lloyd, assigned to me as my nineteen-year-old assistant editor, hinted that we should perhaps join the staff in the commissary. I realized finally that it was the thing to do and that I was embarrassing Russell as well as setting myself up as one of those pushy Americans. I must say it didn't take long for me to accept the custom willingly and soon I looked forward to the daily morning tea.

Lyon and Lloyd at work on "Moscow Nights" at Honslow Studio, 1935.

Russell Lloyd later became one of England's top film editors and worked on several of John Huston's films. Others in the London Films editing department who might be recognized for later accomplishments include Charles Crichton; Henry Cornelius, director of *Genevieve;* Hugh Stewart, producer of the popular Wisdom comedies for the Rank Organisation; Compton Bennett, director of *The Seventh Veil,* who was one of my assistants; Robert Hamer, director of *Kind Hearts and Coronets;* and several others who edited and directed for the many film companies in London that emerged after the success of Korda's operation.

After completing editing on *Moscow Nights,* we premiered the picture quite successfully at the Leicester Square Theatre. Such openings with the big lights, with royalty and other celebrities attending, were new to London, so great crowds gathered to watch the white-tie-and-tailed men and the bejeweled ladies arrive in their chauffeured limousines. I must say I was most uncomfortable in my rented suit of tails, but after several of these openings and other formal functions, I had a dress suit tailored. I got quite accustomed to wearing it, if not entirely comfortable.

My next editing assignment was on *Things to Come* from the H.G. Wells book, *The Shape of Things to Come.* Alex asked Hornbeck to have me recut and polish the first half of the film, since Charles Crichton, the English editor, was fully occupied with the last part, the futuristic sequences, and Alex wished to get the film out as quickly as possible. Crichton later became a director, one of his credits being the most successful *Lavender Hill Mob.* He received acclaim at age 77 for his direction of *A Fish Called Wanda.*

The first part of this H.G. Wells story included very effectively done sequences of the bombing of London, the following pestilence, and the deterioration of the world. In those days the editor cut the sound effects and music tracks as well as the film. He followed the picture through all phases of dubbing, music scoring, negative editing, and supervision of the laboratory processing of the "answer" and first composite prints for theater showing.

When Alex had approved our final editing of *Things to Come,* he set up a screening for Wells. I was most impressed with this little man who always wore a hat high on the top of his head and spoke in a high-pitched voice. When the lights came on after the running, our eyes were on Mr. Wells, of course, because we wanted him to be pleased with our efforts to present his prized creation to the movie world. He slowly rose and paced in front of us for a few seconds, then turned and said, "There is only one thing wrong with this film — it is five years too soon." We all were relieved that he didn't take us apart. Prophetically he was so right, because only five years later, the Germans blitzed London.

A number of Wellsisms remain in my memory from those days, and most of them probably haven't been expressed elsewhere. H.G. attended many of the screenings of the films of his books and was actively concerned with every detail, many of which he didn't understand. But his persistence led to his enlightenment, in some instances at least.

The last scene of *Things to Come* was a composite effect shot of a rocket to the moon. Such scenes often take a long time to perfect — first shooting, then superimposure, lab work, etc. Alex referred to those shots in work as being "in the can." Of course, they would appear in the cut film when finally approved.

After nearly every running of *Things to Come,* Wells would complain that the last shot was missing and ask Alex where it was. Alex always replied, "Relax, H.G., it's all right. It's in the can." The remark seemed to puzzle H.G., and he got increasingly restive. Then one running the final shot appeared on the screen. He jumped up and in his high voice said, "There it is, Alex. That's the shot I wanted and you always said it's in the 'can'." He must have felt that Alex had a new concept of film development that he was not acquainted with.

Another time, Wells was attentively watching a screening when he suddenly yelled, "Stop the film." He turned to Alex and asked who wrote a certain line of dialogue that was strange to his ear. Alex didn't know, so he asked Bill Hornbeck. Bill didn't know, and the script girl spoke up and told Mr. Wells it was his line. Whereupon Wells sat down saying, "A very good line. A very good line. Let's go on." And on they went.

As it turned out, I later got to know H.G. Wells quite well. After completion of *Things to Come,* Bill Hornbeck took a print of the film to New York to show it to the United Artists people and discuss plans for the U.S. release. Because editing on *The Man Who Could Work Miracles* was still in progress, Bill asked that I work with Erich Pommer, Lothar Mendes, and the editor, Phillip Charlot, to expedite final editing for presentation to Alex when he returned from a vacation in southern France.

After viewing the assembly they had effected at that time, I saw great potential in the film and got rather excited about being able to help show Alex a surprisingly good picture. The Wells story was a natural for visual effects and Ned Mann, an American visual effects technician Alex had brought over, had done a magnificent job in my opinion. Ned and his fine department, including Larry Butler of Columbia Pictures fame, had created all the wonderful effects in *Things to Come.*

I found *The Man Who Could Work Miracles* to be slow in developing and unnecessarily wordy and repetitive. Pommer and Mendes responded favorably to my ideas, and we worked together to make the changes. Viewing the results, we all were quite elated and could hardly wait for Alex to see what we had accomplished. Korda returned in a few days, in a good mood, and we projected the film for him. I felt very confident with what was now an excellent piece of film-making. We had really done what we had attempted to do. When the lights came on, Alex turned to us and said we had done a very good job. Of course we were pleased.

Alex then said, "Put it all back."

Deflation set in. I asked, "Why? This is just what this story needed." Alex agreed that it was a good film. He added that Wells was then at his home in Grasse, France, but was expected back in London in a few days to see the film. "He should like it," I exclaimed. And, if Wells didn't like it, wasn't Alex the boss?

At that Alex exploded our expectations by explaining that his contract with Wells stipulated that Wells had complete control over the material used in the final cut and he was certain Wells would never approve the deletions we had made. They had talked in the South of France and Wells had strongly indicated he wanted all the words of the book he had written specifically for the film to be included.

With that, I turned to Charlot and suggested he comply. I walked out and never saw the film again.

I didn't give up completely on *Miracles* because later Alex and I discussed an approach to Wells that might help get at least some of the improvements accomplished. Alex permitted me to discuss any ideas I wished with Wells — and good luck. I suppose it wasn't a matter of life or death for the picture, but I felt quite strongly that it could be improved materially and that some effort to that end was worth a try.

During the time of the final editing, a studio car often returned Mr. Wells to his home en route to my hotel, so I had ample opportunity to attempt to explain to him the value of visual effects to tell the story *without* supplementary dialogue. That chauffeur must still remember today *our* dialogue, which was repeated over and over on several trips. At first I tried to explain film presentation. I pleaded and even begged Wells to accept some of the changes we had made. I have always thought I could be quite convincing in discussing film presentation, but with him I drew a blank. On one trip, I feigned indignity and temper with his stubbornness. The next day Wells delivered to me a well-wrapped copy of his book, *The Man Who Could Work Miracles,* with a note attached that read:

Dear Francis:

This book, with the inserts as noted,

is just as the final film must be.

Yours, H.G. Wells

I still have that book and when I look at it now and then, I often wonder if Mr. Wells had reason to change his attitude at the theater opening, or if in fact he ever saw the finished film with an audience. John Marks and Graham Green, two important film critics, corroborated my views after the premiere.

While the editing staff was finishing *Miracles,* I was cutting a couple of sequences of René Clair's *The Ghost Goes West,* to help his French editor who was behind schedule.

I had little contact with René then, but our paths were to cross two years later.

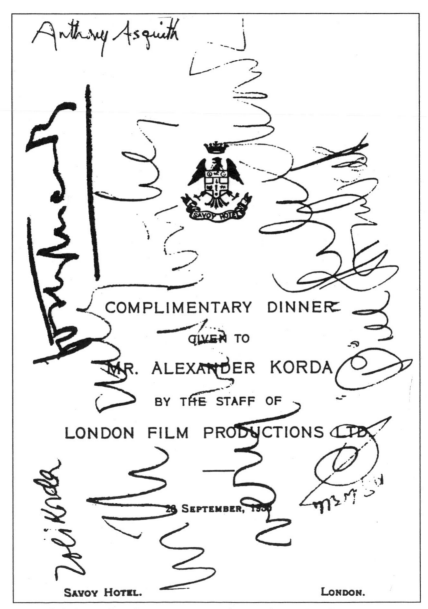

Autographed menu from dinner at Savoy Hotel, September, 1935. The heavy scrawl is Winston Churchill's party signature.

I have a memento of a night in September of 1935 when the staff of London Film Productions Ltd. gave a complimentary dinner to Alexander Korda in celebration of the successes that had come our way. During the dinner at the Savoy Hotel, I acquired the autographs of many of the famous participants on the front of my menu. If you look closely, you can see: at the top left, Anthony Asquith; scrawled on the left side, Winston Churchill; lower left, Zoli Korda; lower right in tiny letters, H.G. Wells; on the right side, Bill Hornbeck; and the big scrawled message across the menu, "With my very best wishes, Alexander Korda."

Many motion picture celebrities visited Alex and the London Films studio. I remember a pleasant chat with D.W. Griffith in the cutting room. I soon understood why he was held in such high esteem in the film world.

As usual in a foreign country, the "expatriates" tend to flock together. When we arrived there were several Americans living in and around London and employed at film studios in the area. To expand the industry quickly and produce quality pictures to compete well in the worldwide markets, the British government was lenient in allowing foreign creative talent to work in England, usually on six-month permits. The local producers were then able to renew these permits easily, which resulted in some rather long terms of employment.

Some American film talents (a few born outside the United States but who had established their careers in Hollywood) who were active in the British film industry during my time there were directors Tim Whelan, Thornton Freeland, Glen Tryon, Roland V. Lee, Sam Wood, Josef von

Sternberg, Raoul Walsh, Tay Garnett, Victor Shertzinger, Jack Conway, Alf Goulding, and William Beaudine; writers Robert Sherwood, John Monk Saunders, Maud Howell, Ralph Spence, and Frances Marion; and producers Joe Rock (who built a small studio in Elstree), Robert Kane (head of production for Paramount in France and later of Twentieth Century-Fox in England), Irving Asher, and Sam Wood.

Mel Templeton of Paramount's estimating department was with London Films in budgeting and later at Pinewood Studios as an executive with the Jack Buchanan Company. Before the labor unions became strict about foreigners, several American technicians worked as cameramen, film editors, effects, laboratory men, and other duties. In 1935, American cameramen in Britain included Charles Van Enger, Glen McWilliams, Phil Tannura, Hal Rossen, Robert Martin, Lloyd Knechtal, and John Boyle. Soon to follow were Harry Stradling, James Wong Howe, Ted Pahle, Charles Rosher, Edward Coleman, Lee Garmes, and Roy Clark.

Several film editors had tenures of various lengths beginning in the late 1920s and early 1930s. Some had returned to the States by the time I started in England, but I recall many who had the opportunity to experience a growing film enterprise in a foreign atmosphere.

As noted before, Harold Young, head of editing for Korda and director of *The Scarlet Pimpernel,* immediately returned to the United States when that film was done. He was replaced by Hornbeck, who had arrived in London at the opportune time. Merrill White had an editing contract company in Elstree and developed Elmo Williams and David Lean, among others. Other editors were Otto Ludwig, chief editor at Gaumont-British Studios; Ralph Dawson and Terry Morse, sent to the Warner Brothers studio at Teddington from Hollywood; and Jack Dennis, Gene Milford,

Harold Schuster, Arthur Hilton, James B. Clark, Frederick Y. Smith, and Jack Kitchen.

Ned Mann, who was in charge of London Film Productions' special effects department, had brought Lawrence Butler as his assistant, and later Paul Morrill as laboratory expert and Edward Coleman as effects cameraman. Lloyd Knechtal was head of the film effects department for the George Humphries, Ltd., Laboratory in downtown London. Technicolor Laboratory was completing a new facility on the outskirts of the city and had imported a few executive supervisors.

Very few Americans came to England on speculation because even with the industry booming it was risky to take a chance on getting a job. Most arrived with a specific assignment, and all seemed to enjoy the opportunity until it became necessary to return home.

With all these Americans around, those at the same studio or living in the same areas or those just naturally compatible seemed to drift together often for dinners, parties, and travel. Bill Hornbeck and I were in constant contact at the studio and lunched together nearly every day, so I was indoctrinated quickly into some of the local idioms and customs. Bill led me to his tailor, and to several restaurants and quaint pubs.

Ann and I were fortunate to meet Jane and John Mock, who had followed us to London. John was appointed story editor for Twentieth Century-Fox covering the European territory. Jane and Ann met by way of letters from mutual friends in Los Angeles. Through the Mocks we met many other interesting English and American people, and the four of us spent many happy hours together.

Lee and Ruth (Hall) Garmes were among the first Americans to arrive after we had become settled. Alex had sent for Lee, a prestigious Hollywood cameraman, to photograph some tests for *Cyrano* and *I, Claudius,* which were then scheduled for production. I believe Alex had Charles Laughton and Merle Oberon in mind for the leads in *I, Claudius,* and Laughton and a promising young actress, Vivien Leigh, for *Cyrano.* He wished to make extensive tests of them for costumes, makeup, etc. Vivien was then in a successful play in London, and Alex had great hopes for her as a film actress. At his request I saw the show and quickly concurred with his opinion of her potential. Later I got to know her quite well and found her to be a most delightful person.

We soon learned that the Garmeses shared our desire to see as much of the English countryside as possible before our terms expired, so we decided to hire a car and drive on weekends together to cover the country, using London as the hub of a wheel and the spokes as different directions for as often as time and money would allow. It's natural, I presume, for one to be concerned about taking advantage of any available time in order to consume the fruits of such an opportunity for sightseeing. As it developed, Ann and I had nearly four years of this concern and, fortunately, we used it fully.

For our first Christmas vacation in 1935, we decided to go to Paris. It would be my first visit, but Ann had been there with her grandmother some few years before. We allotted a big bit of our savings, $75, which, believe it or not, was enough for travel, an inexpensive hotel, and reasonable meals for a three-day stay. Perhaps a Bal Tabarin girlie show would also fit in. The dollar stretched out very favorably in Europe at that time.

We checked in at the Rond-Point Hotel near the Champs-Élysées, a comfortable, well-located little place that was recommended by Bill Hornbeck. We had a most satisfactory dinner the night of our arrival at the nearby Café le Cabaret. By coincidence, as we were about to leave we heard the unmistakable laughter of Ned Mann. We tried to leave without acknowledging his presence because with our limited budget I honestly didn't want to get involved in a big night on the town. Ned had a reputation as a big spender, and I knew I would be way outclassed if we were to join with him for any activity in Paris. He was with his wife, Cora, and his assistant, Larry Butler — three friendly and nice people.

But I really wanted to sneak into Paris for my first time like a country boy to taste its excitement, and possibly return later with better financial backing to explore the best it had to offer. Just being there exhilarated me greatly. I'm sure many Americans share the excitement Paris instills in the first-time visitor. So I wanted to explore its attractions in my own way.

But Ned spotted us, and reluctantly we responded to his vociferous command to join his party for coffee or liqueur. We were practically forced to accept his hospitality for the next three days. When he found out it was my first visit to Paris, he announced that he had just won about $2,000 at Deauville and it was his primary responsibility and pleasure to introduce Ann and me to the wonderful attractions of the City of Lights. When I declined with thanks, stuttering that I had budget limitations, he most forcibly announced that there would be no further discussion. We were from then on his guests in Paris, and we were not allowed to pay for anything except our hotel bill at the Rond-Point where, incidentally, the Manns and Butler were also staying.

We'll be forever beholden to Ned Mann for the delightful memories of that nonstop night-and-day montage of events. For instance, one morning about 3 A.M. as we were quietly watching the world go by while having a nightcap on the walk at the Café de la Paix, Ned abruptly announced that he had decided the reason Paris was so exhilarating was that the government hired crews of men to spray Spanish fly around the city constantly! At the time, I believed him.

Would that I could replay those scenes today. I want Ned Mann, wherever he is in God's Heaven, to know our everlasting gratitude for his kindness.

After that pleasant experience, we made other short visits to the continent whenever work permitted. One was in April of 1936, when production was curtailed while we were preparing for a move to a new studio that was just about finished at Denham, a village on the outskirts of London. This junket included Italy, one of the countries we had not yet visited.

Of the many interesting places we saw, we were especially impressed with Venice. At that time, Italy was at war in North Africa. Mussolini was trying to satisfy a desire to establish a stronghold on that continent. One day in Venice we had an exceptionally good lunch at Harry's Bar, a well-known hangout. Our expressions of satisfaction to Harry prompted him to invite us to a special dinner that evening which he would be pleased to prepare for us if we wished. Of course we wished, and we agreed upon a time to arrive.

We were told that this "Harry" had taken the American owner's name to use for business purposes since he was a partner. There is also a successful Harry's Bar in Paris, so I don't blame "Harry" for enjoying its prestige.

That afternoon when we were in a men's shop buy-ing a Borsolino (a fine Italian hat), suddenly all hell broke loose. We heard sirens, whistles, and shouts from people rushing by the shop in apparent panic. As the shop owner started to close the door, I asked what all the excitement was about. I wanted to buy another hat while I was there. He told us to get out quickly and go back to our hotel, where we would be safe. Soon Mussolini would be address-ing the nation over loudspeakers in the towns, and he wanted the people to drop whatever they were doing and listen to his announcement.

We complied. The hotel people explained that good news about the Ethiopian campaign was expected, which was the cause of the commotion. The worry was that we might be suspected of being English, who were hated because of the sanctions they had imposed upon Italy. Excited youthful gangs could rough us up.

Since we were about to enjoy a special dinner, we sat still until time to leave. We left at the appointed hour to go to nearby Harry's, where we saw our Harry in full Fascist regalia leaning on the closed door. I hardly recognized him with the long tassel hanging from his cap, wearing riding trousers and boots, and with an indifferent attitude. A pity I didn't have my camera.

He saw our concern and said it wasn't every day that Italy captured a capital and annexed another country, so in celebration he wasn't about to open up that night. A small twist of fate.

In mid-1936, London Film Productions, Ltd., moved to its beautiful new complex near Denham, Bucks, even though some construction was still in work. The company

London Film Productions studio near Denham. The former stables became the cutting rooms.

The back lot of the studio.

had purchased a wonderful old country estate called The Fisheries. Several stages were complete, and the new laboratory was about ready for business.

The cutting rooms had been fashioned from the renovated stable area. The main offices and commissary were temporarily located in the impressive old manor house. The back lot was real English country with many acres of tree-lined lanes and open country vistas. The Colne River (creek) flowed slowly through the estate and fed a lovely lake back of the house. It was an ideal area for filming.

My first assignment at Denham was to edit *Rembrandt,* starring Charles Laughton, Gertrude Lawrence, Elsa Lanchester, and Roger Livesey. Alex directed as well as produced it. The cameraman was George Perinal, a great French artist who had photographed several of Alex's previous films.

About the time *Rembrandt* was scheduled to start, Robert Kane, who was on the lot to produce *Wings of the Morning,* asked for me to edit that picture and work closely with him during production. I had to decline because Alex wanted me on the set with him during the principal photography of *Rembrandt.* Since he had the multiple tasks of running a large new studio as well as producing and directing an important property, he wanted all the backup he could get. I was elated that he felt I could be of assistance to him.

Bob Kane sent to Hollywood for Harold Schuster, who had been a film editor for Twentieth Century-Fox, and Harold brought his assistant, James B. Clark. *Wings of the Morning* starred Anabella, Henry Fonda, and Leslie Banks. The famous Irish tenor, John McCormack, sang a few songs in the picture, the first Technicolor film to be made in

England. The director was Glenn Tryon, who had been preparing for some time before Schuster arrived.

Kane had occasion to needle me often in the months to come because, as he put it, I wouldn't accept his offer. Shortly after shooting started, Tryon became ill and Bob asked Harold to take over as director, an important opportunity for him. Clark became editor, a break for him also.

The film was well received, and I admit I reflected at times about this twist of fate, a thing that happens to so many of us in this amazing business where it seems decisions that affect our destinies for the rest of our lives are made continuously, either by ourselves or by those over whom we have no control. *Wings of the Morning* was the beginning of Harold's successful directing career in England and Hollywood. Jimmy Clark had many subsequent editing assignments and later several fine feature and television directing credits.

Rembrandt, however, was a most interesting adventure for me, since it was my first full-time experience on the set, and Alex was very cooperative and appreciative of my suggestions.

I suppose the greatest excitement came through my close contact with the cast. It was Gertie Lawrence's first film and she seemed alert and amused at the procedures, especially by Charles Laughton's attitude toward his work. Gertie displayed a fine sense of humor and was loved by the crew members. She joked a lot and enjoyed needling Charles for his serious and painstaking attention to the details of acting. Perhaps her humor helped Gertie get over any nervousness in this new medium, but I felt she also just fully enjoyed film-making. Elsa Lanchester was very cooperative and competent.

I recall one day while we were staging the long Saskia sequence in which Rembrandt delivered the impressive eulogy to his wife, Saskia, before the assembled burghermeisters, Alex had rehearsed the scene at some length, then turned the set over to the photographer, George Perinal, for lighting. This preparation took quite some time because of the size of the town hall and the number of people involved. When the set was ready for the cast Charles was not available. Alex called for him a few times with no response. I had a hunch where he might be, and sure enough I found him at the far end of the stage pacing the floor and mumbling his lines. I told him Alex was ready to shoot, and he replied that he wasn't yet in the mood for the scene. Without hesitation he kept right on mumbling and walking back and forth. Later, when he did get into the mood and reappeared on the set, Gertie gave him "what for" to the amusement of everybody but Charles and, I presume, Alex.

Whatever Laughton felt it was necessary to do must have been right for him, because his reading of the scene was really great and was applauded by the crew. He had considerable confidence in his ability at this time and justifiably so, in my opinion. However, we later had a bit of a confrontation when I was editing the picture.

One day after putting the Saskia sequence together, I checked it with my assistants in the projection room to see what changes, if any, I wanted to make. Alex had covered Charles's close-ups with wonderful reaction shots of the burghermeisters and waitresses, which heightened the effectiveness of the speech. I had purposely cut to Charles for emphasis only, and I thought this technique allowed the scene to build to a strong impact.

By coincidence, as we left the projection room, Charles stepped down from the booth. He had seen the sequence through the portholes and it was obvious that he was not happy with what he saw. He made a remark about the lack of close-ups of him and turned away. I knew I would soon hear from Alex, and sure enough, in a few minutes, he asked me to come to his office.

As I also had expected, Charles was sitting there waiting to hear Alex confront me with his wishes for editing changes. Alex repeated Charles's complaints, and I suggested that Alex first look at the sequence and then we would discuss what was best for the picture. He agreed, and I never heard another word. I never changed a cut, and to my gratification, after the big London premiere the critics commented favorably, especially on the Saskia sequence.

I didn't know if Charles Laughton ever forgave me for my approach to the film. But a few years later when I was back in Hollywood as film editor on *Intermezzo,* David Selznick called my cutting room and asked that I run a reel or two of the cut film for Charles Laughton and his wife, who were visiting the studio. When Laughton and Elsa Lanchester came around the corner, he looked up and recognized me. He stopped suddenly and shouted, "Oh no!" I laughed and he actually greeted me quite cordially.

Because *Rembrandt* was a recognized artistic success, credit was given to the great contributions of the photographer, George Perinal, and the art director, Vincent Korda. Vincent was different from his brothers in many ways. In appearance he looked more like a Marx brother than a Korda brother. He was completely unconcerned about material things except as they affected his work, but even there the budget elements needed to be carefully supervised. The end seemed to justify the costs, and money especially seemed an enigma to him.

As an example, the comptroller at the studio (a Scot; it seemed most of the British film money people were Scots) told me that Vincent hadn't picked up his weekly paycheck (cheque) for months. When Vincent was asked why he didn't claim his due, he said he didn't need it because Alex always gave him a fiver whenever he needed it. I could well believe that Alex absent-mindedly doled out enough to satisfy his brother's needs.

Some time later the bookkeeping department put pressure upon Vincent to pick up his checks. Vincent often went for advice to his good friend, Ned Mann, with whom he worked closely in the design and execution of miniatures and mechanical and film effects. When Vincent asked Ned what to do with these checks, Ned advised him to deposit the money in the bank and told him which one he used. Ned thought Vincent would ask him to go with him to the bank when he was ready, but Vincent went straightaway alone.

In England, a depositor must be "recommended" as a customer, so when the bank asked for a reference before it could open an account for Vincent, he couldn't comprehend the refusal of his money. He picked up his checks, went back to the studio, and gave the checks to Ned to do what was necessary. He had lost any further interest in the whole ordeal. Ned immediately took Vincent back to the bank and got the matter settled.

It appeared that Vincent's favorite pastime was to be in Paris, and he went there as often as he could. On our first visit to Paris, while we were making the rounds with Ned Mann, I recall seeing Vincent about 2 A.M. one morning, sitting at a large round table in La Coupole, a popular Montparnasse watering place, pleasantly surrounded by a bevy of young, good-looking women. I still remember clearly how he sat rigidly in his chair, his hat (it was always there) on top of his ample hair, as he gave us a little wave of recognition and a knowing smile as we were being ushered to our table.

That was his delight — just to be in Paris. When he was asked about the attraction as compared to other European cities, he naively exclaimed that there was no other place where you could look out of the window in the morning and see the beautiful Eiffel Tower while sitting on the "can." It's a viewpoint, one has to admit.

Vincent later married Gertrude Musgrave, an actress. I recall seeing their baby son in his cradle in their home. He is now Michael Korda, the well-known author of a book on his family, *Charmed Lives,* among others.

Zoltan Korda was another cut of the jib. He was the youngest and perhaps least talented of the three. However, he had several good directing credits including the successful *Sanders of the River* starring Paul Robeson, which he made in Africa with hundreds of natives in the cast. He was quite adept at handling them and got some excellent results on film. He also directed *The Drum* and *Four Feathers.*

Some of us felt that Zoli resented the influx of foreigners into England's film world because he believed their presence curtailed to some extent his importance and his ability to contribute to what Alex was trying to accomplish. Perhaps he was justified because, for example, when Robert Flaherty was making *Elephant Boy* in India, and there was some concern about the production, Alex asked Bill Hornbeck if I could be available to go there and help get things straightened out. When Zoli heard about the idea, he insisted on going himself. Since Zoli was available, Alex concurred, and Zoli spent some time in India with Flaherty, and later brought Sabu and his elephant back to Denham for added scenes.

The development of an important artistic contribution to increase production quality in film-making was being advanced by two employees of London Films, Pop Day and his stepson, understudy, and assistant, Peter Ellenshaw. They were among the reasons for Vincent Korda's acclaim for art direction in such films as *Things to Come, The Drum, Four Feathers,* and *Rembrandt.*

Glass shots, the art of painting backgrounds and/or additions to sets or scenes to be placed strategically before the cameras and photographed simultaneously with live action, were most difficult to create. Very few artists at that time would or could adapt to the rigid requirements or even understood the fundamentals of this artistic approach.

I believe there was no one in the business more capable and effective in this art than the late Pop Day. Ellenshaw learned well and later became perhaps the best known and most respected of all these artists, as evidenced by Walt Disney's selection of him to work on his films in Hollywood. Peter and I were to renew our association when he was assigned to paint several glass shots for *The Great Locomotive Chase,* a picture I directed for Disney. Peter also contributed great work on *Love Bug, Darby O'Gill and the Little People, 20,000 Leagues under the Sea,* and *Mary Poppins,* for which he won an Academy Award.

Peter has supplemented his film work with a successful career as perhaps the most prominent American painter of seascapes and landscapes. I have followed his artistic endeavors with interest.

Shortly after the Korda studio was settled in Denham, Ann and I moved from our hotel at Marble Arch to an apartment (flat) in Ealing Village, then a large new complex off Hanger Lane in the suburb of Ealing. Since it was about halfway between Piccadilly Circus and the studio, and near a subway (underground) stop, it was a convenient location.

Once we had somewhat larger quarters we did some small entertaining at home, having dinner guests once in a while. One day at the studio, I was bragging to Tony Asquith and Teddy Baird, his assistant, about Ann's ability to make one of my favorites, Mexican chile and beans. Even though I warned these two Englishmen, used to their country's rather tame fare, of the heat of the chili peppers, they insisted upon testing it. The results were surprising — they had seconds and thirds until it was all gone. A few days later, they asked for a retake, so apparently they didn't experience any Mexican heartburn.

Donn Tatum, a friend of Ann's brother from Los Angeles, was a student at Oxford University so we had him as a guest one evening. After dinner he drove us on a hairy tour through the rough Limehouse District near the London docks, the hangout of the tough, the no-gooders, and the criminals. It was scary and dark, with narrow, crooked streets affording ample opportunity for the uninitiated to get lost. And that is just what happened to the three of us packed in Donn's little two-seater. I still don't know how he brought us home safely out of that jungle, even with the help of a couple of bobbies who were concerned about our presence in the area of their responsibilities. Our guide was the Donn Tatum who later became president of Walt Disney Productions.

At a later time Donn's younger brother, Warde Tatum, visited the Ealing area and we enjoyed having him join us one evening. He was later known as Warde Donovan, actor and one-time husband of Phyllis Diller.

Margot Asquith had shown an interest in seeing our flat. We set an evening for dinner, which turned out to be one of the foggiest days we had yet experienced in England. When Margot was late in arriving, I went out to see if I could guide her through the fog to our door. I soon found her and her chauffeur not far from our entrance, but hopelessly lost. For those uninitiated to the pea-souper it is difficult to believe the lack of visibility it can cause. One time I actually stretched out my arm in front of my face and could not see my hand! We have been in Piccadilly Circus at noon, when from appearances it could have been midnight.

While preparing *Rembrandt* for dubbing, Bill Hornbeck had given me the script of *Knight without Armour,* written by Frances Marion from the James Hilton book, as my next assignment. I suggested a few small story changes to Alex, who had hired Jacques Feyder, the French director who had made the very good *Carnival in Flanders,* and thought it best to wait until Feyder started preparing so he could be consulted on script changes.

My assistant editors on *Knight without Armour* were the same as those on *Rembrandt* — Peter Bezencenet, whose sister was then Mrs. Ernst Lubitsch, and Compton Bennett. Compton or Bob, as he was most often called, was a quiet, soft-spoken chap with great artistic talent that needed stimulating to get the exposure it deserved. His work as an advertising artist apparently wasn't satisfying so he had turned to film as an outlet. In my opinion, his directorial expression in *The Seventh Veil* proved that he was most deserving of the opportunity. He came to the United States after its success to direct *King Solomon's Mines* for MGM.

When Jacques Feyder arrived I tried to get through to him about some script ideas, but he seemed interested only in shooting the script as written. Bezencenet had gone to school in Switzerland and spoke very good French, and Feyder had very little English, so I asked Peter to run dailies with Feyder, who could then convey any comments to me. That plan worked fine except Jacques never had anything to convey. Then one day, well into shooting, Feyder really teed off on Peter about something I had said to Alex about the film.

Indeed, while running the dailies with Alex each afternoon, I had suggested adding a line to help eliminate some episodical problems in the story. Alex asked Sir David Cunningham, his assistant, to suggest the change to Feyder on the set. A couple of evenings later, Peter came back to the cutting room and wanted to know what I had done to Feyder. That afternoon when I ran the dailies I realized the line I had suggested was not included, and Alex expressed his annoyance to Feyder for not complying with his request. Feyder took his resentment at me out on Peter. When I asked Peter where Feyder might be he said perhaps at the studio bar. I went to the bar to speak with Feyder.

Here I must digress a bit to mention that during one of our visits to Paris we had met Harry Stradling, a very fine cameraman who had recently received much praise for his photography of *Carnival in Flanders* for Feyder. We enjoyed the Stradlings' company in Paris quite often. I had suggested Harry as cameraman for *Knight without Armour,* and Alex hired him because the film's stars, Marlene Dietrich and Robert Donat, deserved the best.

During one of our Paris pub crawls, Harry had told me that the continental producers and directors were a different breed of cat from the Americans he was used to. If I was ever associated with them and if there was any controversy, he said, I must firmly stand my ground if I believed I was right. Weakness was fatal and strength respected.

I recalled Harry's words as I looked for Jacques. This was my first test of his theory. It is not my nature to fire up too hot or to face a fight too quickly, mostly because I'm a coward at heart. But I realized that if I were going to get along with this director during cutting and dubbing, I had to settle the issue right now.

Jacques was just about to leave the bar when he saw me motion for him to come outside. I didn't want a scene in front of the bartender. Jacques was a dapper dresser, and I remember vividly that he was wearing a black coat with a chinchilla collar and picking up his black Homburg as I appeared. I could tell by his expression that he suspected what I was there for. Outside, I lit into him in a quiet but firm way to indicate my displeasure at his not being man enough to discuss his quarrel with me instead of my assistant. I further jabbed him with the fact that my suggestions were made only for the good of the picture and that our personality differences had no interest to me since I was working for Alex and not him. I strongly suggested that in the future he deal directly with me for the good of all concerned.

He stared silently at me for a few moments, probably absorbing the points made by translating them into French or just realizing that perhaps I did know what I was doing. Then he grabbed my hand and said in his very broken English, "Francees, I sank you for coming to me. We now understand each ozzer. Sank you." From then on I could do no wrong for him, and eventually he seemed most appreciative of my editing and dubbing of his film. C'est la guerre!

While still finishing *Rembrandt* I tried to keep up with the shooting on *Knight Without Armour* so Alex could evaluate the production to date. As we projected the cut film we were all impressed with Feyder's staging of the crowd and production scenes. Harry Stradling had done a marvelous job of matching scenes often shot in the ubiquitous fog to those photographed in near sunshine. I still don't understand how, under such circumstances, he could expose film that would be intercut and match so well in the final printing. As a matter of fact, the end result was a beautiful film that received extremely favorable comments for photographic excellence.

I don't believe Marlene Dietrich was ever photographed better, and she became a great booster for Harry. She praised his work to David Selznick, who later sent for him to photograph *Rebecca*. Stradling's potential has been substantiated by the acclaim for his credits in photographing *Funny Girl* (Academy Award), *Hello, Dolly!*, *Pygmalion*, *The Picture of Dorian Gray* (Academy Award), and *My Fair Lady*, to name a few.

Several projects that had been in preparation for some time began to take shape. In 1937 activity at Denham picked up considerably, with *Rembrandt* finishing; *Knight without Armour* shooting; *Elephant Boy* back at the studio for added scenes; and Mayflower's production of *Fire Over England* produced by Erich Pommer, directed by William K.

Howard, starring Flora Robson, Laurence Olivier, and Vivien Leigh.

Troopship, produced by Erich Pommer, directed by Tim Whelan, and photographed by James Wong Howe, was one of the smaller-budget pictures planned that year, along with *Wings of the Morning.*

Josef von Sternberg started directing *I, Claudius* in February, 1937. After six weeks, shooting had to stop when Merle Oberon was hurt in an automobile accident. It never resumed because Charles Laughton had another commitment, so the whole project was written off. I believe some of the footage was salvaged and used later on television.

Roland V. Lee directed *Love from a Stranger* with Ann Harding and Basil Rathbone. All in all it was a busy year at Denham, but few realized that by the end of 1937, there were 23 active studios in the country. No wonder so many foreigners were needed to supplement the English artists and technicians in that explosive industry.

One of the casualties of this influx was an ambitious project that Winston Churchill was working on at London Films, *The Life of Marlborough.* Since Churchill's political party was not in government at the time, Alex hired him to research and write the screen treatment for the big-budget production. They were good friends and all of us had ample opportunity to meet and respect him. Churchill was a regular guy who loved to chat about any subject, especially films.

When Alex started to assemble the creators and crew for this picture, the British government, under pressure from the fast-growing Association of Cine Technicians, requested replacement of most of the foreigners with Englishmen. Alex refused to comply because he wanted the most experienced and competent personnel available on such an important production. When the government's labor authorities became adamant, Alex scrubbed the picture forthwith.

One ponders the frightening possibility that if this twist of fate had not happened, Winston Churchill might have had a successful career in the motion picture business and England might have lost a great leader.

REEL 5

A CHANGE OF STUDIOS

About the time I was finishing with *Knight Without Armour,* I began to get overtures for jobs at other companies that were feeling their oats in the expansion of the English film industry. I was attracted to the offers of much more money and responsibility. London Films couldn't do better than Bill Hornbeck as supervisor and it didn't appear that I could advance beyond film editor there. So the only avenue for my career to advance would have to be else-where.

Since production at London Films was at a stand-still, I thought it was a reasonable time to make a move without leaving Hornbeck short of help. I discussed this with him and he agreed that it was to my benefit for the present, but Alex Korda had told him that when things picked up, I was expected back if I was available at the time.

I accepted an offer from Jack Buchanan Produc-tions, located at the nearby Pinewood Studio in Iver Heath. I received a substantial increase in salary, and the respon-sibility of organizing a department and supervising the editing of a four-picture program to start, with an increased yearly production schedule to follow.

Pinewood Studios is also located at an old attractive country estate with a large manor that accommodates of-fices, commissary, club rooms, and living quarters. It is a well-planned independent studio complex with ample ex-pansion and backlot areas.

Mel Templeton, the former Paramount Studios budget and estimating expert who had been brought to England by London Films, became business affairs executive for the newly formed Jack Buchanan Productions at Pinewood. He's the one who arranged for me to join the company.

In October, 1937, my first exposure to production at Pinewood was *Break the News* with the French comedy director René Clair as producer and director, music by Cole Porter, starring Jack Buchanan, Maurice Chevalier, and, at the start, Adele Astaire (Lady Cavendish), Fred Astaire's sister, who was to make a comeback in this picture. For personal reasons she withdrew before shooting started, and June Knight was cast as the female lead.

I ran into script problems with my first Buchanan film similar to those with the Korda-Feyder picture. Clair, like Feyder, was adamant about shooting the script as he had approved it. Although I found him to be most polite and gentlemanly, he was firm in his story convictions and method of shooting. For example, he seemed reluctant to overlap shots to cover scenes — that is, to repeat action and dialogue in other angles that allow fluidity in editing. Undershooting seemed to be a European method, unlike the American approach of ample coverage, which sometimes becomes too ample. For editing purposes, I prefer the latter.

Because of his great reputation from *Le Million, Sous Les Toits de Paris, A Nous La Liberté,* and *The Ghost Goes West,* it is difficult to fault a René Clair. However, experience had taught me to be concerned about the results of a project where one person exercises complete autonomy over all elements and decisions in the complexities germane to the making of a motion picture.

My firm conviction is that the better films are the result of the contributions made by many good creative minds. By this I mean that, if at all possible, the scriptwriter, director, and editor all should be encouraged to make suggestions to the producer or producer/director about the script and story while the script is being written. Collaboration by creative talent is usually helpful in all stages of production. Of course, the director is in charge during principal photography, and he usually is receptive to thought-out suggestions, whether or not he uses them.

The film editor on René's picture, Fred Wilson, complained to me that he was unable to influence René and asked to be reassigned because he felt he was just a mechanic functioning under orders on every cut. I placated Fred: "Your time will come. Just be patient."

Phil Tannura, the American cameraman, seemed to meet the same attitude from the director when he tried to make suggestions for covering during shooting. But he resisted frustration, as good technicians must learn to do.

One evening René presented his cut to some friends in the studio projection room. Among those invited were Charles Laughton, Erich Pommer, and some others from London Films and local producing companies. The picture did not go over well. The next morning I was called to René's office. He evidenced some embarrassment and great concern as he asked for my help. A bit late, I thought, but I suggested we project the picture reel by reel to see what could be done.

As I suspected, the timing was off in many scenes, and other obvious changes in cutting were needed. But these cuts were minor compared to what I felt was more important for story clarification — script problems. The film needed added scenes and bridges to plug some holes in the story line and to strengthen continuity faults that had been apparent to me in the original script — and which I had brought to René's attention before shooting started.

After running only five reels and listening to my suggestions, René announced that he must return to Paris and suggested I do what I could to improve the picture — without being too drastic. When I was finished I should call him. By this time Jack Buchanan was doing a Shubert show in New York and Maurice Chevalier was on tour in North Africa, so we would have to fix the film problems without them. I told René there were limitations to what could be done without the appropriate film coverage, but we could try to improvise some tricks to get results impressionistically without the stars.

René's seeming new confidence in my ability to take over his film completely was a bit puzzling to me until Fred told me René had recently heard about my background, especially my experience with Mack Sennett. René was an admiring student of Sennett's contributions to the film business. I guess this awareness of my training through Sennett and his realization that the film needed attention justified turning it over to me.

Ralph Spence, a noted writer from Hollywood, was working on another Pinewood project, and when I called him for consultation we developed some ideas for shooting scenes to cover the gaps in *Break the News*. Lloyd Knechtel was the photographer and I directed the scenes Ralph and I had improvised. When we had completed all the post-production work and received the answer print, I set a showing at the suburban Croydon Theatre and so advised René.

On the night of the showing, the Croydon manager enthusiastically announced that the audience was about to see a film by the famous René Clair, starring Jack Buchanan and Maurice Chevalier. He prepared the crowd well and the showing was surprisingly successful. René was ecstatic with the results. I never learned how the picture did in general release because we were back in the United States by the time it was released. It would be hard to believe it got the acclaim of that preview because theater managers seldom warm up their audiences before each showing.

René later told me that I was the first one to teach him the value of timing, and the experience had been important to him. I still prize his praise.

Other Buchanan Productions we completed around the same time were *Smash and Grab,* directed by Tim Whelan; *The Sky's the Limit,* directed by Lee Garmes; and *Sweet Devil,* all produced at Pinewood.

In 1938 the Hungarian producer Gabriel Pascal had been successful in arranging the rights to film George Bernard Shaw's *Pygmalion.* This was an acknowledged coup by a foreigner with nothing to offer but courage, which seemed to impress Mr. Shaw. At any rate, the deal was set and the next concerns were problems of financing, production procedures, direction, and crew assignments.

One morning, Mel Templeton asked me to come to his office to discuss a problem. There I met a most impressive, big man, of conservative dress and manner. He was J. Arthur Rank, a wealthy British flour miller who had supported some religious film projects. Now he was interested in theatrical production and would provide backing for Pygmalion. Templeton and Rank asked my opinion on the selection of a director for *Pygmalion.* Leslie Howard would star and co-direct, with Wendy Hiller and Wilfred Lawson as the other leads. With that cast I suggested Anthony Asquith as the most qualified director, and Asquith subsequently accepted the offer.

Then Mel wanted to know if I could handle the editing. Since I was involved with the four Buchanan pictures, I felt I couldn't do justice to a project as important as *Pygmalion*. I recommended a promising young editor who had been with Merrill White's editing company in Elstree — David Lean.

One morning a few weeks after shooting had started on *Pygmalion* I arrived in my office to find David slumped in a chair and wearily waiting for me. I soon found out he was experiencing a problem similar to what I'd been through with Feyder and Clair. Pascal was criticizing everything David did when they ran cut material, and wouldn't listen to reason from his editor. Lean thought Pascal really didn't understand editing and was covering up by shouting his displeasure.

I knew how to handle this communication problem. I recommended that David take a quick, strong approach and make it clear he was standing by his cutting work. I even suggested some profane dialogue he could use in rebuttal when he knew he was right.

A few days later, David was again in the office when I arrived, this time looking happy. He confirmed that my advice had worked like a charm. He could now do no wrong, and all was harmony between him and Pascal.

David Lean's career took off after that. *Pygmalion,* recognized as being well directed and edited, was very successful at the box office. The great montage sequence that underlined the strenuous education of the girl was David's work, and he soon was rewarded with the opportunity to direct, first as co-director with Noel Coward on *In Which We Serve* and then on his own. His great achievements in the years to follow are many and include such films as *The Bridge on the River Kwai* (Academy Award),

Great Expectations, Hobson's Choice, Lawrence of Arabia (Academy Award), *Dr. Zhivago,* and *Ryan's Daughter.*

After I had wrapped up and delivered the Buchanan pictures I needed a long vacation from the pressure and responsibility of getting Buchanan's films in as good shape as possible under some trying conditions. My resistance was reaching a danger point.

When I discussed my plans with Mel, he said I could take a month off but I must be back after that because he wanted me to be part of a large new production company being planned. He wouldn't tell me any more about it, but insisted I would be very pleased with the company's plans for me.

Ann and I had planned a three-month car tour of the continent beginning in April, 1938, so I told Mel I would be in touch after the first month. He told me to relax and not worry about the future. I had no problem about the relaxing part, but some concern about the future.

Ann and I were financially and mentally prepared for a three-month vacation on the continent, and we expected it to last unless, for good reason, Mel called us back to London sooner.

We drove our fully packed English Ford to the English Channel to take the auto ferry to France, and our first stop was Paris. After a few days, we drove south to Cannes on the Mediterranean Sea. By now we were in the right mood to make the most of the time we had. With no preplanned schedule to follow, it was a euphoric time.

Even the escapades of Adolph Hitler and his recent annexation of Austria didn't seem to dampen our expectations until we arrived in Rome via Mentone, San Remo, Genoa, and Livorno. The city was preparing for Hitler's arrival with decorated streets, Nazi flags, and welcome signs. The Fascist and Nazi movements suddenly became real to us.

Mussolini decorated Rome for Hitler's arrival, 1938.

Palazzo Vecchio embellished with Nazi flags in honor of Hitler's visit.

Hitler's arrival brought a strange atmosphere to the city. It appeared that he continued to impress Mussolini and the people with the importance of their membership in the Rome, Berlin, Tokyo Axis. Strict security was enforced, at least it was supposed to be. Hitler and Mussolini were being escorted together, in open cars, to and from meetings in different locations night and day. As foreigners we were told to remain in our hotels at certain times when they might be passing by.

Bill Hornbeck came to Rome to be with us for a few days during a breather from his activities in London. He brought his well-equipped Leica camera and was keen to photograph the events and the parades.

One day, the caravan was expected to pass along the wide avenue past the Victor Emmanuel monument. The three of us were in the crowd, along the street in a good position to see the action. However, armed Fascist soldiers were lined up facing the observers to see that no photographs were taken of the two dictators as they passed. However, as soon as their car approached, the soldiers all turned to see it, leaving Bill free to shoot as many pictures as he wished.

One cold night, Ann, Bill, and I were in a crowd overlooking another street, expecting the leaders' car when I felt a tap on my shoulder. I turned to see a large man motioning to my overcoat pocket, which was suspiciously bulging with my 8mm motion picture camera. I showed it to him but, not satisfied, he asked me to operate it. After I wasted a few feet of film he left, convinced I was not carrying a bomb.

Another time, we watched a parade of German soldiers marching behind their military band and followed by Italian troops. In the crowd along the street was a group of

Bill Hornbeck's surreptitious shot of Mussolini and Hilter in their caravan through the streets of Rome.

Italian troops on the march in Rome.

attractive young girls waving at the men as they passed. The Germans paid no attention, but when the Italians saw the girls they fell out of step and bumped into each other. The following Germans and the people watching expressed their amusement, of course. What do they say about the Italians? That they're lovers, not fighters?

Coincidentally, I ran into Tom Geraghty, a well-known Hollywood writer, who was in Italy on an assignment to work on a script about the life of Mussolini. I had known him through his two sons, Maurice and Jerry, who had been in high school when I was. Both boys also became film writers. A daughter, Carmelita, was a promising actress at the time.

It was surprising that Tom remembered me, since I had been in his house only a couple of times. He had been a fan of Hollywood High sports. One day Jerry had come to school with a $20 bill his father had given him to take the baseball team to the fun pier at Venice Beach. We all appreciated his generosity.

Tom asked what I was doing, and when I brought him up to date, he said the director who expected to be on the Mussolini film, if and when it was made, was ill and it was possible that he could get me to do it if I was available. I told him I appreciated his interest, but Ann and I were on our way to Vienna in a couple of days. If something should happen he could reach me there at the hotel. Nothing happened and, as far as I know, the film was never made. At least I enjoyed the meeting.

Bill stayed with us through Naples, Vesuvius, Pompei, Sorrento, and Capri before returning to London. Ann and I went north to Austria via Florence, Bologna, and Padua. We bypassed Venice because, as I previously noted, we had already enjoyed an exciting stay there.

Entering Austria, we saw our first example of Hitler's oppression. A large sign on the border over the highway directed traffic to run on the right side of the road throughout Austria. Hitler's order changed overnight what had been the practice of driving on the left for years. I can't imagine the number of accidents this directive caused. But this was minor compared to the depression of a people suffering from the whims of a despot named Hitler.

After a short stay in Austria we were looking forward to Budapest. I had told a friend with Kodak in London that Ann and I expected to be in Budapest sometime during our tour, and he had said he would be there at a certain time for a business meeting. He had suggested we call the office if we were in Budapest at the same time because he would like to show us the city.

We drove along the Danube River past beautiful country and arrived in Budapest, one of my favorite continental cities, in good time. After checking in at the St. Gellert Hotel, I called Kodak and found my friend there. He invited us to have dinner with him that evening. He took us to the Arizona Club, famous for its entertainment and food. It had a large round dance floor and good music. In cubicles lining the walls, high above the floor, were good-looking naked girls. Apparently they were just for decoration. We enjoyed the evening.

The contrast in attitude and dress between the people in Budapest and those in Austria was striking, of course. The people in Budapest were free — for the present.

Incidentally, much later, in 1986, we visited Budapest with a Directors Guild of America group during a tour of Iron Curtain film studios. It was an exchange deal with their government-controlled production companies. Though I had retired, I had retained my DGA membership so I was entitled to join the expedition. Ann and I took advantage of the opportunity, which was well worth while.

I asked our guide in Budapest about the Arizona Club, and he was obviously surprised that I had known it so many years before. He said the building was still there but was occupied by another enterprise. Considering the situation then, we thought Hungary was in much better shape than the other communist countries we visited.

To return to our 1938 trip, from Hungary we drove to Germany in spite of warnings of possible trouble. However, we were treated well there, as we had been in Austria. I suppose the Nazis hoped tourists would carry a favorable impression to our various regions. Good luck!

While driving through Germany, we saw signs of the most fortified country ever: airplanes constantly overhead, soldiers in training everywhere, Hitler haranguing thousands of his troops in Nuremburg, horse-drawn caissons rumbling by our hotel all night on their way to the Ruhr, Jewish stores so indicated by the "Jude" painted on their fronts, greetings of "Heil Hitler" accompanied with the upraised right arm of the mandatory Nazi salute.

We went from Munich to Berlin to Hamburg and on to Esbjerg, Denmark, where we picked up Pat and Ellie Brett, English friends who were joining us for the Scandinavian part of our tour. This would complete our three months of traveling, and the four of us would return to England together. Or so we thought.

After we had been to Copenhagen, Stockholm, and Oslo, somehow Mel Templeton located us at Dallen, a small village in southern Norway. We were en route to Bergen to meet our ship back to Newcastle, England. He sent a cablegram requesting me to phone him as soon as possible. When I called, he said we should cancel our plans to return to England because the company was not yet fully formed and it would be much easier to obtain a labor permit for me if I were out of the country when they applied for it.

Fun is fun, I said, but I can't afford to live like a king in retirement forever. Mel said the company would pay all our expenses until it could officially send for me, which would be soon. With this apparently pleasant twist of fate, we got a boat out of Bergen to Rotterdam, then drove to Paris. The King and Queen of England were scheduled to visit Paris, so we decided to drive south and miss the crush and excitement their visit certainly would cause. Pat and Ellie left us in Paris and returned to England.

Ann and I drove south to the Spanish border, hoping to see a bit of Spain. We could not get our American passport stamped for admission because the Spanish civil war was still going on. So we decided to stay a while at a pleasant hotel at Hendaye Plage, a pleasant village at the Spanish border near Biarritz, until London was ready for our return.

After about two months of relaxing at Hendaye, we began to worry about the lack of instructions to return to London. We returned to Paris, where our bank in London forwarded money weekly to the branch on the Champs Élysées near the apartment that friends had arranged for us to rent not far from the Arc de Triomphe. I phoned nearly every week to see how much longer this life of luxury could last.

It lasted until the Munich crisis in September. Suddenly, Paris was filled with the near panic of mobilization, with owners of businesses and banks fleeing daily. I phoned to tell Mel that we were leaving on the first boat that would take us and our car from Calais to Dover. Actually we got the last one.

So the three months of vacation turned into six months and 10,000 miles of travel. The details of our tour of the continent added up to an education and a sense of involvement in the history of our times: Hitler's move into Austria; the Hitler-Mussolini meetings while we were in Rome; the German troops moving by our hotels at night toward the Maginot Line; the French mobilizing to the Maginot Line while we were in Paris.

In London I met with Mel Templeton and Jack Buchanan, who had recently returned from New York. I assumed it was Jack's company that was being reorganized, and no one indicated anything to the contrary. They accepted the necessity of our return from the continent and asked me to be patient while things were still being arranged. Mel also agreed that my expense money would continue until the company could legally pay me a full salary.

Travel and living expenses were amazingly low in Europe in those days. During our 10,000-mile tour through ten countries in our 65-hp English Ford, Ann and I did everything that appealed to us — staying at the best hotels as long as we wished, eating at the best restaurants, or deciding to stay in cheaper and more atmospheric places. And our expenses for six months amounted to less than $5,000. Today one could easily spend that in six days.

At another meeting, Mel asked about the highlights of our vacation. We could happily return to Paris to live, I told him. I recalled saying to Ann one morning as we strolled down the Champs Élysées, "If Heaven is half as good as this, that is where I want to go." Mel said he had never been there

(Paris, that is) and because of my enthusiasm, he must immediately take off a few days and see those sights.

His sights were aimed mainly toward the revues. The topless shows held particular interest and he wanted me to suggest the best one for his first visit.

Mel was rather reserved, vain, and well-groomed, but his sense of humor possessed a strange naiveté and shyness, which I liked him for. With mischievous intent, I suggested he might appreciate the thrill of an introduction to the most popular of the girlie acts in Paris at the time. His first stop should be a place Ned Mann introduced us to, 25 St. Apolline. I told Mel that Ann and I thought it was the best of its kind in the city and that he should be pleasantly satisfied with the display.

By coincidence René Hubert was also going to Paris, which would be helpful since Mel didn't speak French. René was the leading wardrobe designer in Europe at the time and a regular guy. I had known him at London Films and, since he was then doing a film on the lot at Pinewood, I cornered him and told him about my plan. He readily went along with it and later I learned the results through René.

At 25 St. Apolline, as with a New York brownstone, there was a first door at the top of a few steps from the sidewalk, then a short vestibule to a double door that swung inward. René escorted Mel to the door, stepped back, and allowed him to proceed. As Mel opened the inside door, suddenly twelve pretty young women swarmed at him, all yelling, "Me! Me!" They were adorned with earrings, necklaces, and high-heeled shoes but absolutely nothing in between.

Mel nearly fainted with shock, René said, but soon gathered his frayed reserve enough to be escorted to a nearby table. I didn't press for further information.

25 St. Apolline was one of the better houses in Paris (I was told, of course). Ann and I enjoyed dropping in once in a while for a beer or champagne. It was fun to sit at one of the small tables that lined the mirrored walls of the rather large reception area and watch the action. If things were slow, we would invite one or two of the girls to join us for a drink. Since we spoke a bit of French, we found them to be interesting company, and they seemed to enjoy our conversation while they were waiting for more pressing business. It was fun to watch the compulsive vanity of those waiting; they couldn't resist the temptation to stop at a mirror, pose a bit, and adjust their beads. There was nothing else to adjust.

This kind of exposure when we were in our 30s may explain why many of us don't get too uptight about the seemingly frantic and rampant sexual attitudes of the young. One can't help but shrug, so what else is new? What's new now is AIDS, which, of course, must be dealt with forcefully.

The scene has many interpretations. It depends upon where you place the camera.

Sir Neville Chamberlain's "Peace in Our Time" speech didn't lessen the war scare. Armies feverishly dug trenches in the London parks, installed antiaircraft guns (mostly wooden), and distributed gas masks and other supplies throughout London. In spite of this panicked preparation and our observations of Germany as a huge armed camp, many of our English friends bravely remarked, "If Hitler starts anything we will finish him in six weeks!" Oddly, when we returned home, we heard the same remark — including the six weeks time period — from Americans about the Japanese threat. There should be a lesson here somewhere.

Denham Studio, 1938, sand-bagged in preparation for coming war.

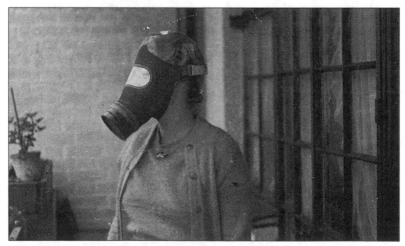

Signs of the times — Ann Lyon trying out the mandatory gas mask, London, 1938.

By Christmas, 1938, I was still on the hook of this new phantom company. Mel Templeton had become no less secretive except to say my position was definitely in the offing. But we had had enough of being patient, especially with the war atmosphere escalating, and we were ready to return to the States. Mel understood and said he would send for me as soon as final details were worked out with the government. The cable would probably be waiting when we arrived home. What patience and faith he had!

We enjoyed a last Christmas dinner in London with Margot Asquith and Tony Asquith at their home. It was the finale of many, many wonderful memories of nearly four years of association with some of the greatest people one could be fortunate enough to meet in this world.

P.S. Sometime later, when the United States was in the war and I was stationed with the Army in New York, I coincidentally met Joe Rock, an American producer, in an elevator when we were both going to the Office of War Information. Joe had built a small studio in Elstree, a suburb of London, where I had last seen him.

During our discussion, he expressed surprise to see me in New York and asked why I hadn't taken the job in London that had been held for me for so long. When I confessed my ignorance about plans afoot in 1938. Joe said he thought I knew, as he did, that I was to be assistant in charge of all production for the newly formed J. Arthur Rank Organisation.

It took a war to cause the twist of fate that prevented that intention from coming true.

P.P.S. Mel Templeton must have been told not to inform me about these plans until they were officially settled. I can't believe he was trying to get even for the way I introduced him to the Paris revue.

BACK HOME AND
A CHANGE OF UNIFORM

Gone with the Wind was well into production and *Intermezzo* was in the preparing stage at the David Selznick International Studio in Culver City when it was time to get back into action on my home grounds in 1939.

William Wyler was assigned to direct *Intermezzo,* starring Leslie Howard, Ingrid Bergman, and Edna Best. The timing of our return proved favorable because I was given the editing job and the chance to work with David Selznick and William Wyler, both prestigious professionals.

Before the picture started, however, there seemed to be some differences between the two geniuses. Wyler left the studio and was replaced by Gregory Ratoff. Ratoff, who had been a successful actor for some years, had directed only one film, at Twentieth Century-Fox. Coincidentally the cameraman was Harry Stradling, who had been brought from England to photograph *Rebecca* for Selznick and Alfred Hitchcock. When *Rebecca* was postponed, Harry was assigned to *Intermezzo,* a job he was rather reluctant to accept for some reason.

After about a week of shooting, Selznick assigned me to help Ratoff with his setups and camera moves and to make any suggestions that might contribute to better action and coverage. Ratoff seemed rather upset to think that Selznick felt he needed the help. For a few days it was slow going for me, but with Stradling's cooperation Ratoff soon realized that I was only trying to help make him look good. In a short time he began to rely upon me to help plot out the

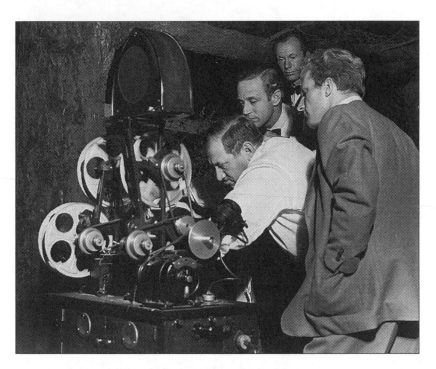

Gregory Ratoff, director of Intermezzo, *Leslie Howard, star and associate producer of the picture, and technicians at film viewing machine used to help the director match scenes that will be next to each other in the finished picture.*

At work on Intermezzo,1939. Francis D. Lyon is second from the right.

scenes, and later he often took off early (usually to see Darryl Zanuck) and asked me to finish out the day's work. Nothing could have made me happier because I was getting experience in directing an important production.

Stradling also had some differences with Selznick and soon he took off for England. He was replaced by another outstanding photographer, Greg Toland, who had been under contract to Samuel Goldwyn for some time. He picked up where Harry left off and was extremely coopera-tive and fast. As a matter of fact, when I was cutting later, I couldn't tell one man's work from the other's. For some added material and inserts I shot after the editing was finished, I was assigned George Barnes, also a prominent and excellent cameraman. All three have now passed away after unusually successful careers in motion picture pho-tography.

When *Intermezzo* was finished I was scheduled to direct some second unit material for *Rebecca,* but before it started I was called to Twentieth Century-Fox and offered a cutting job there. Since I had heard that the Selznick company was closing down after *Rebecca,* I decided to accept the opportunity to work with Darryl Zanuck, who seemed to value good editing. And there might be an opportunity to direct for him some time. Ratoff had praised my work to Zanuck and suggested he give me the editing job on Greg's next film, which was to start in a few days. Darryl probably acquiesced to humor his good friend at the time.

During my first year at Fox, I edited *Daytime Wife* and *I Was an Adventuress,* directed by Ratoff; *Four Sons,* directed by Archie Mayo; and *The Great Profile,* John Barry-more's last film, directed by Walter Lang. All had impor-tant casts and were well-done productions, so I had an interesting year. I even enjoyed Zanuck's autocratic approach to all phases of film-making.

Zanuck was amazingly alert. No detail seemed to get by him. I never understood how he could keep in mind the intricacies of six or eight scripts in work, the same number shooting, and eight or ten films in the cutting rooms. One day I went to his office to ask his permission to make a cutting change that was not indicated in the script. One did not waste Zanuck's time, so I started talking as I entered his office, and before I reached his desk some distance away he gave his approval without even looking up from the script he was reading.

Another time Zanuck was walking down the hall with the heads of advertising and distribution when he saw me waiting. He stopped to ask what I wanted, and when I explained another cut I wished to make, he approved and went right on talking to his companions. In neither case did he ask what picture, what sequence, or my reasoning. The approval was instant from my brief description. When we subsequently ran the first cuts, he readily acknowledged the wisdom of the suggestions.

Zanuck appreciated the quality of cutting and demanded tight, smooth first cuts so that further editing was, for the most part, deletions or additions of material in the interest of the film's entertainment values.

Gregory Ratoff left the Fox lot to direct an independent picture at Columbia Studios, *Adam Had Four Sons,* and asked me to supervise the editing and work with him on the set. Since I didn't see any directing prospects for me in the offing at Fox, I accepted. The picture starred Ingrid Bergman, Warner Baxter, and Richard Denning, and introduced a newcomer, Susan Hayward. Again, I got valuable set-time directing experience and was pleased about being able to contribute to a successful film. Ratoff was always most appreciative of and complimentary about my contributions, so my confidence for directing was being gradually strengthened each time I worked with a production crew.

As time went on there were more editing jobs but no feature directing assignments. I always hoped for the big break and believed it would appear one day. Wishful thinking perhaps, but I was never unhappy about cutting, because there is a lot to be accomplished in the editing process. Editing can be satisfying, especially if one is allowed to be creative. Sometimes the opportunities presented themselves in unexpected ways.

One of those unexpected twists of fate was initiated at Pearl Harbor, Hawaii, on December 7, 1941.

After our entry into World War II, many motion picture people soon became active in making films with the armed services and government agencies. Such prominent personalities as Jack Warner, John Ford, Darryl Zanuck, Emmanuel Cohen, George Stevens, and Frank Capra headed units responsible for assignments deemed necessary and contributory to the war effort. They in turn rapidly recruited creators and technicians from studios and the independent fields to help in supplying the vast need for orientation, training, combat, information, and propaganda films throughout the country and in the worldwide theaters of war.

Film-making for the war effort soon became a tremendous enterprise requiring great numbers of personnel, equipment, and millions of feet of raw stock film for the continually increasing military and national responsibilities.

Some participants from Hollywood and other production areas found themselves in familiar activities, but in new surroundings and wardrobe. Others were given assignments quite foreign to their past experience and responsibilities. This miscasting of film people was not unusual, particularly in the military, and I suspect the same was true for personnel from other endeavors who were drawn into the armed services.

I believe my wartime experiences contributed materially to my preparation for the opportunity to direct feature films.

My first contact with an agency active in the war effort was early in 1942. A section of the Office of Emergency Management, located in New York City, asked me to help in a program of informational films that had been requested by the White House. The O.E.M. was a direct responsibility of the President, who had funds at his disposal to use for any emergency that was not covered by any other agency. Thus, he had rather broad powers to cut corners and, for example, to present a particular message to the people by film in the most expeditious manner.

The O.E.M. was soon absorbed by the new Office of War Information, headed by Elmer Rice, and the unit I was in became the O.W.I.'s Bureau of Motion Pictures, headed by Lowell Mellett and his assistant, Arch Mercey, both very efficient executives.

As my first major assignment, I was asked to make a film called *Colleges at War* as quickly as possible, to inform the American public about the necessity to keep certain students in college while others were left subject to the draft. I had suggested to the Washington office that there was a need for such an explanation, so they started me at once researching the project.

I quickly discovered that the contributions to the war by the institutions of higher learning were considerably more varied than I had anticipated. Both classified and unclassified subjects were offered by many colleges, particularly those specializing in aerodynamics, electronics, chemistry, and engineering. Crash courses were given in languages such as Russian, German, Japanese, and Chinese. A new military government school was organized at the University of Virginia, and Navy training centers were established at several colleges. Black and women's colleges all offered some specialty that related to the war program; many taught familiar subjects with some significant differences.

After I had selected fourteen representative campus locations by geographical, architectural, and educational variances, and assembled the crew and photographic equipment, we started on tour in a station wagon and equipment truck. Without taking a day off, we covered a great area of the country in a short time.

Following completion of the shooting, I edited, wrote the narration, and delivered the finished print to Washington for approval. It received enthusiastic acceptance and I was further gratified by several favorable critical reviews of it in the newspapers. From the material photographed, I made two additional films — a longer version called *Campus on the March* and *Negro Colleges at War* — both of which received distribution in the informational and educational 16mm fields. *Colleges at War* was widely distributed to the domestic and foreign theatrical markets.

Since this was my first chance to contribute entirely on my own at the O.E.M., it was satisfying to feel that I had accomplished something. I was asked to transfer to the main office in Washington, which was housed in the building known as "Mellett's Madhouse" at Fourteenth and Pennsylvania. Actually, by then I was euphoric because it was a promotion and a chance to be in the center of wartime activities in the Capital.

My new duties were varied. The use of vast quantities of raw stock film by the armed forces and Hollywood left a limited amount for other producers. One of my responsibilities was to review all applications for raw stock film allocation other than military and Hollywood, and to forward my recommendations to the War Production Board, which had final say on all material allocations. We were to judge the merit of each film request based upon our assessment of unnecessary duplications in the commercial area.

Another responsibility was to supply crews and equipment for photographic coverage at the White House whenever President Roosevelt requested it. I found an O.S.S. unit headed by Navy Captain John Ford available, efficient, and security-cleared. With so many film units then in the Capital it was seldom difficult to comply with the periodic requests for photographic crews.

The Signal Corps Army Pictorial Service, headquartered in the huge Pentagon building, had requested that our bureau, since it was a major civilian film unit, attempt a consolidation of all film libraries that were cataloging film that could be interchanged for war-effort use. The project of compiling a Central War Film Index with the cooperation of all services, military and civilian, fell to my office.

At first I enjoyed the challenge, but later I wished it had fallen somewhere else. Almost without exception, the leaders of government and military film units showed no interest in assigning away any part of their bailiwicks. Empire builders to the fore! We kept at it, making several attempts to gain headway but, although it was a reasonable idea, it proved to be a lost cause.

After a few months of interesting activity in the excitement of wartime Washington, I began to get the irresistible urge to join my friends in uniform. I had hoped to get into the creative fields of picture-making as a military man, where my efforts would be more defined and visually expressed. A naive hope at best!

Given my many contacts with military personnel through my O.W.I. activities, it was reasonable to expect easy access to any openings in the service units, which were voraciously seeking usable manpower, especially in the early days of the war. A good friend from Los Angeles, Herb Hazeltine, then an officer in the Navy Bureau of Personnel, was politely urging me to apply for a commission. He claimed he had at least three billets open for men of my qualifications.

More or less as a lark, and to get Hazeltine off my back, I filed the Navy papers with the understanding that I was not obligated to accept it if a commission should be granted. I took the physical and ended up with glasses and the information that I was somewhat color blind. Both things, I thought I could have done without.

One of the requirements to accompany the Navy application was a few letters of character recommendation from acquaintances of some standing. On the following page is one I value highly from a prominent screenwriter friend.

As it turned out, I was also urged by Capt. Douglas Yates of the Signal Corps Training Film Production Laboratory at Wright Field, Ohio, to file for a commission to expedite production of the Air Force training film program. I passed this physical with no problem.

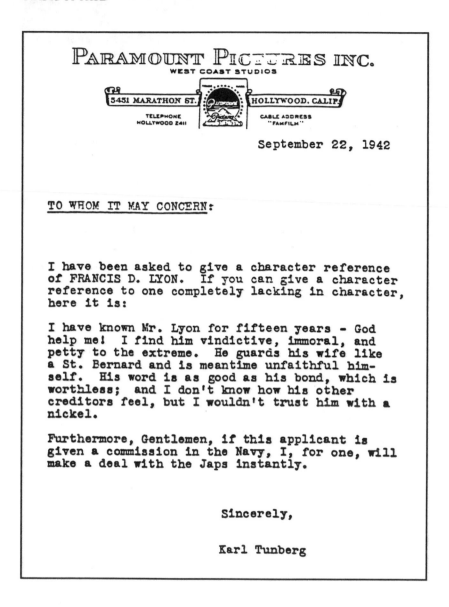

PARAMOUNT PICTURES INC.
WEST COAST STUDIOS

5451 MARATHON ST.   HOLLYWOOD. CALIF.
TELEPHONE   CABLE ADDRESS
HOLLYWOOD 2411   "FAMFILM"

September 22, 1942

TO WHOM IT MAY CONCERN:

I have been asked to give a character reference
of FRANCIS D. LYON. If you can give a character
reference to one completely lacking in character,
here it is:

I have known Mr. Lyon for fifteen years - God
help me! I find him vindictive, immoral, and
petty to the extreme. He guards his wife like
a St. Bernard and is meantime unfaithful himself. His word is as good as his bond, which is
worthless; and I don't know how his other
creditors feel, but I wouldn't trust him with a
nickel.

Furthermore, Gentlemen, if this applicant is
given a commission in the Navy, I, for one, will
make a deal with the Japs instantly.

Sincerely,

Karl Tunberg

About the same time, I was beginning to get unexpected rumblings from my draft board in Beverly Hills,
California. Soon I found myself in a race for time — against
the day either the Signal Corps or the Navy commission
would come through; against the day the draft board would

invite me to an induction ceremony (if I passed that physical too); against a decision to remain a civilian with the O.W.I., since Arch Mercey had said that I was one of only four requests he was submitting to the White House for deferment from military service. I honestly believed that I could contribute more to the cause by remaining at my O.W.I. desk, but I couldn't shake the crazy notion that I should be in a uniform. However, I definitely preferred one that had bars or braid on it.

As a story in itself, I am presenting the correspondence with my friendly draft board that I have resurrected after all these years.

October 21, 1942

Local Board 247
Selective Service System
426 N. Canon Drive
Beverly Hills, California

        Att: Mr. Milton H. Berg

Dear Mr. Berg:

        This will notify you of change of address from 35 West 45th Street, New York City to Office of War Information, Bureau of Motion Pictures, Room 2205, 1400 Pennsylvania Ave., N. W., Washington, D. C.

        After making three pictures for the Office of War Information, Production Unit, in New York, I have now been transferred to the headquarters office in Washington to work on the planning of Government films, handle the allocation of restricted raw stock film and direct Washington scenes needed for Government films.

        When I am permanently located, I will forward my home address.

                Sincerely,

                Francis D. Lyon

ORDER REFERRING REGISTRANT TO ANOTHER LOCAL BOARD
FOR PHYSICAL EXAMINATION ONLY

INSTRUCTIONS

1. The local board of the registrant shall prepare this form in triplicate. It shall send one copy to the local board to which it refers the registrant for physical examination only, together with three copies of Form 200 filled out by it in the manner provided in paragraph 337 of the Regulations, send one copy to the registrant, and place the third copy in the registrant's cover sheet.

2. The local board to which the registrant is referred for physical examination only shall retain the copy of the order which it receives in its files, together with the third copy of Form 200 when completed. The local board mentioned below will notify you when and where to appear for this physical examination

SELECTIVE SERVICE
LOCAL BOARD No. 247
426 NORTH CANON DRIVE
BEVERLY HILLS, CALIFORNIA (STAMP OF LOCAL BOARD)

October 28, 1942
(Date)

To LOCAL BOARD covering: 1400 Penna.Ave.,N.W.,

Washington, D.C.

In accordance with section XX of the Selective Service Regulations you are requested to have

Francis   Davis   Lyon
(First name)   (Middle name)   (Last name)

Order No. 91   , whose present address is   Room 2205, 1400 Penna.Ave.,N.W.

Washington, D. C.

physically examined.

Member of Local Board.

D.D.S. Form 208   U. S. GOVERNMENT PRINTING OFFICE   16—28881

November 2, 1942

Selective Service Local Board No. 247
426 North Canon Drive
Beverly Hills, California

Attention: Mr. Milton H. Berg

Dear Mr. Berg:

I have just received the D.D.S. Form 203 stating that I will be notified when and where to appear for my physical examination. From this form, it is not clear to me whether I am reclassified from 3A to 1A, or whether I am soon to be reclassified to 1A. I have checked with the Local Board of this district and find they have no word of my case.

On stating that I am married, living with my wife, who is wholly dependent upon me, I was advised that perhaps this was only a check-up to see how many men might be physically capable of being classified to 1A if and when necessary.

This Local Board said they have 400 or 500 single men still to be called, but of course, they are not acquainted with the situation in Beverly Hills.

In order to bring you up to date on my case, I further wish to advise you that some days ago I filed application for commission in both the Army and Navy, at their requests. Should you find it necessary to reclassify me to 1A, I wish to request deferment until these applications are acted upon. Therefore, because of the exigencies of mail delivery and the time involved because of distance, I ask now that this letter serve as a formal request of appeal for deferment.

Sincerely yours,

Francis D. Lyon

1400 Pennsylvania Ave., N.W.

Selective Service   December 1, 1942
Local Board No. 247
426 North Canon Drive
Beverly Hills, Cal.

Dear Sirs:

      Supplementing my notification of appeal by letter
of November 30th, regarding my reclassification from 3A to
1A, I hereby state reasons for requesting 3A classification.

      While in New York, I presented an idea for a film
to be used in promoting public morale, and was assigned to
write and direct a series of pictures that are now being released throughout the country and abroad.

      After the change from Office of Emergency Management
to Office of War Information I was asked to transfer to Washington to work on the planning of Government films, to act as
Technical Advisor on film problems here in Washington and to
establish and organize a Central War Film Index System among
other duties. My work here is technical in nature, but requires certain administrative abilities in dealing with Government officials and high ranking Army and Navy officers.

      In the film business, it is difficult to get people
with a sound technical background as well as capable administra-
tors to do the kind of work I am doing here in Washington.

      However, I only state the above to show you my position
here and not to ask for deferment or change of classification
for occupational reasons only.

      Further, since I was approached by both the Army and
Navy to file papers for commissions to fill definite jobs that
require someone with my qualifications, it seems only reasonable
that you should grant me time for these commissions to be acted
upon. It is being done here and in New York as I have been told
so by a local bo rd. They feel that it is only reasonable to
grant this time where manpower is needed for definite War work.
I should hear favorably from the Army about my commission within
the next three weeks.

      For the above reasons, can't you grant me two months
of 3A classification?

                        Sincerely,

                        Francis D. Lyon

TO: Francis Davis Lyon
Rm. 2205, 1400 Pennsylvania Ave., N.W.
Washington, D. C.

FROM: Local Board #247

SUBJECT: Classification

        This Local Board, in session December 7, 1942, declined your request for further deferment.

        Therefore, you will be mailed an induction notice within the next two weeks for our next induction, January 4, 1942. Kindly let us know by return mail whether or not you wish to be inducted in Washington, D.C.

        Very truly yours,

FOR VICTORY
BUY
UNITED STATES
WAR
BONDS
AND
STAMPS

J. Paul Herdman, Chairman
Local Board #247

        1400 Pennsylvania Ave., N. W.

        December 17, 1942

Mr. J. Paul Herdman, Chairman
Local Board No. 247
426 North Canon Drive
Beverly Hills, California

Dear Mr. Herdman:

    Your letter of December 11th to Mr. Francis D. Lyon, has just arrived in his absence, since he was called out of town on business for a day or two.

    As soon as he returns he will answer your letter.

        Sincerely,

        Lillian Lovitz, Secretary

Dear Mr. Herdman:

In reply to your letter which arrived December 17th, kindly be advised that I would prefer to be inducted in Washington, D. C.

Sincerely,

Francis D. Lyon

ORDER TO REPORT FOR INDUCTION

The President of the United States,

To ___Francis_____Davis_____Lyon_____
(First name)   (Middle name)   (Last name)

Order No. __91_____

GREETING:

Having submitted yourself to a local board composed of your neighbors for the purpose of determining your availability for training and service in the armed forces of the United States, you are hereby

notified that you have now been selected for training and service in the ___Army_____
(Army, Navy, Marine Corps)

                                                    426 North Canon Drive
You will, therefore, report to the local board named above at _Beverly Hills, California_
                                                              (Place of reporting)

at __6:15 a.__ m., on the _____4th_____ day of ____January____, 19__45.__
(Hour of reporting)

This local board will furnish transportation to an induction station of the service for which you have been selected. You will there be examined, and, if accepted for training and service, you will then be inducted into the stated branch of the service.

Persons reporting to the induction station in some instances may be rejected for physical or other reasons. It is well to keep this in mind in arranging your affairs, to prevent any undue hardship if you are rejected at the induction station. If you are employed, you should advise your employer of this notice and of the possibility that you may not be accepted at the induction station. Your employer can then be prepared to replace you if you are accepted, or to continue your employment if you are rejected.

Willful failure to report promptly to this local board at the hour and on the day named in this notice is a violation of the Selective Training and Service Act of 1940, as amended, and subjects the violator to fine and imprisonment.

If you are so far removed from your own local board that reporting in compliance with this order will be a serious hardship and you desire to report to a local board in the area of which you are now located, go immediately to that local board and make written request for transfer of your delivery for induction, taking this order with you.

Member or clerk of the local board.

D. S. S. Form 150
(Revised 7-13-42)

Mr. Daniel Feder
Local Board No. 247
426 North Canon Drive
Beverly Hills, California

Dear Mr. Feder:

In response to the Order to Report for Induction for Francis D. Lyon, I wish to advise that Mr. Lyon was commissioned Captain in the Army on December 22nd and has already gone to Wright Field, Dayton, Ohio. However, you may have already been informed of this by the War Department.

Sincerely,

L. Lovitz, Secretary

Perhaps it is amusing now — but it wasn't then.

The situation at the Wright-Patterson Air Force Field Film Unit was unique in that the personnel assigned to make films for the Air Force was the Army Signal Corps. Like the other military film units, it was hurriedly assembled from scratch into a conglomeration of civilian and military people charged with the responsibility of delivering requested film projects as quickly as possible. They were supposed to research, write, photograph, edit, and deliver the subjects without delay, because the need to save time was especially important in the early days of war preparation.

When I reported to Colonel Horn, the commanding officer at the lab, he assigned me to head the editing department with authority to do whatever was required to get the pictures finished and delivered. The bottleneck seemed to be in editing and he would sign any orders needed to expedite the process.

My first move was to meet with the film editors to get their opinions about the operation and suggestions for improvement. It appeared that I had inherited a competent department with such editors as Elmo Williams, later producer of *Tora, Tora, Tora* among others and production head of European Twentieth Century-Fox; Lou Lindsay, later a Music Corporation of America talent agent; John Sturges, who edited the films he directed for the Air Force and later became one of Hollywood's best; John Sheets, later supervising editor of the Lassie series; Desmond Marquette, an Emmy winner; Tom Scott, Les Orlebeck, and other proficient technicians. Since these guys were so competent, there just had to be something beyond their control that deterred getting the work out. There was.

A few military project officers and supervisors assigned to films in the heat of expansion were over their heads in a field they were not equipped for. But for them it was play time. Some had never seen a moviola before and were fascinated by the new toy. They were having fun with film, so they kept their projects in the cutting rooms to experiment as long as they could get away with it. The professional editors were not able to complete the cutting to their satisfaction because they were continually making changes for the few incompetents who tenaciously held on to their authority.

My second move was to deny admission to the cutting room to anyone without my permission. This way I could determine who the detractors were and take away their influence so we could fulfill our obligations. Needless to say, I wasn't popular in some areas, but the pros understood my motives and cooperated fully.

At any rate, we delivered the films and got an efficient operation into effect in short order. It was interesting to note the change in attitude toward me by some of the incompetents when they began to get commendations from the field for the fine products they were credited with.

Production began to flow smoothly. Enthusiasm for accomplishment was obvious, and the general morale looked up. The men were pleased with the reception of their efforts and looked forward to their next assignments.

The roster of professional film-makers at Wright-Patterson was impressive, when one considers the competition for talent among the services. Capt. Douglas Yates, the personnel officer, had done an excellent job of recruiting from civilian and military backgrounds. Many civilian pros volunteered for duty who could have remained safely at their peacetime endeavors.

Among the dedicated contributors from Hollywood I can recall were: Charles Grayson, Everett and Devery Freeman, Charles Lederer, Earle Snell, Mauri Grashin, Melville Baker, Sumner Lyon, Stanley Rau, Lynn Riggs, William Saroyan, Richard Goldstone, Ewing Scott, Jerry Sackheim, Cy Feuer, Herb Stein, Marshall Grant, Mel Tucker, Ted Hirsch, Hiram Brown, Dave Mathews, and Charles Haas.

Things were going too well. Soon there were waves on the water foreboding ill for the future of the unit. Repeated visits by Air Force brass from Washington led to rumors of some kind of imminent change. Enthusiasm began to wane. It seemed clear to some of us that the shop could eventually be closed.

Some of our best men were sent overseas. I became so depressed that I even filed an application for Military Government Service, not only because I felt I was equipped for it, but I had a strong belief that I could do more abroad than I was allowed to do at posts like Wright Field. Fortunately, perhaps, my request for transfer was denied by our C.O. after being accepted by the Military Government Service. If he hadn't turned me down, I would probably have been running some occupied village in Europe for the Army long after the war was over. I should have known better than to ask for anything in the Army.

Actually, some of us were prophetic because before long the Air Force brass decided to disband the unit and establish a film-making post of its own at the Hal Roach Studio in Culver City, California. It was soon dubbed Fort Roach. Several Signal Corps officers and men were transferred to the Air Force and shipped to the coast while others were ordered to the Signal Corps Photographic Center at Astoria, Long Island, for reassignment. Civilians had to fend for themselves. I never understood how the Air Force selected which men went where, because no pattern was evident in the transfers.

Perhaps the move was made in the interest of economy, but I seldom heard of that excuse being used in all-out wartime. I know it took the starch out of a lot of conscientious men for a while until they could gather some momentum again in other assignments.

There is one virtue of most motion picture people with which I am continually impressed — pride of accomplishment. Even in the armed services, where it is often difficult to perform to one's best ability because of elements beyond the individual's control, many fine film creators and technicians were able to rise above some ridiculous obstacles in order to do a professional job. We see this trend evidenced with consistency in most Hollywood productions, and one can seldom complain of any lack of effort from those who spend most of their lives in this great industry.

During the break-up my orders were to report to Astoria. There I was told by Col. Emmanuel Cohen and Lt. Col. Anatole Litvak that orders were being cut for me to report to Col. Frank Capra in Hollywood. Capra was making the famous *Why We Fight* series — including *The Battle of Britain, The Battle of China, Prelude to War, Divide and Conquer.* He was close to Gen. George Marshall and spent much of his time with the top echelon at the Pentagon.

I was pleased to return to California and join the Capra group. Again, I was assigned to handle the editing department but not the editing in this case. Major Bill Hornbeck had been with Col. Capra since the start of his unit and was actually the officer in charge of editing. He worked directly with Capra on all projects. That left me with the business and organizational problems.

As one would surmise, there were some talented men in the Capra unit. At the top were Robert Riskin, Col. Sam Briskin, and Litvak. Others assigned with various rank and ratings were Ted Geisel (Dr. Seuss), Claude Binyon, William Holman, Stuart Heisler, Henry Berman, William Lyon, William Claxton, Sam Beetley, John Huston, Merrill White, Jack Ogilvie, Anthony Veiller, Buddy Adler, Robert Stevenson, and Meredith Willson.

After about two months Major Bill Holman was ordered to Astoria to head the management of film functions. The next thing I knew, old "Yo-Yo" Lyon was ordered back to Long Island and assigned as Holman's assistant.

En route, I stopped at the Pentagon to visit with the C.O. of the Army Pictorial Service, with whom I had worked closely as a civilian on the Film Library Index problem. He casually remarked that I must have some value to the Signal Corps Photographic Center because they (Holman, of course) insisted that he change orders already cut for me to go overseas, so I could report back to the New York Center. It turned out that the orders he voided were for me to head a photographic unit in the first D-Day landing group. What did I say about the twists of fate?

Upon reporting to the C.O. of the Astoria post, Col. Barrett, I was sent for assignment to the C.O. of Production. He was Lt. Col. Emmanuel Cohen, former head of production at Paramount Studios in Hollywood. There I also met the Adjutant, Capt. Robert Benjamin, a pleasant and efficient officer who later became president of United Artists. At Cohen's office I was told to report to Major Holman for assignment — Evers to Tinker to Chance.

Under Major Holman, I was assigned to be Officer-in-Charge of the Film Branch, which included the Editing Department, Central War Department Film Library, Negative Cutting, Film Research, Newsreel Department, and the Security Laboratory. A lot of headaches, and still no real creative opportunities.

At that time, the S.C.P.C. was the largest of the military training film factories. It was staffed by military and civilian personnel from all over the U.S.A. For the most part, it was well organized and did a creditable job of producing and distributing films for many military purposes.

At Astoria, Army Combat Photographic units were staged, trained, and assigned to fighting forces to secure film coverage of all army activities during the war. As the war progressed, film records of the numerous battles and campaigns were viewed, assembled, edited, and filed.

A security film processing laboratory was necessary because much of the incoming film was classified as high as Top Secret. It was difficult to get enough people cleared to view this classification, let alone to process it.

The superintendent of the Consolidated Film Lab in Hollywood before joining the Signal Corps, Capt. Ted Hirsch, was assigned to head and organize this army lab, which was located at the DeLuxe Plant in New York City. The Film Branch supplied him with personnel, mostly inexperienced in this field. However, in an amazingly short time Hirsch had his plant operating efficiently.

At the Central War Department Film Library in Astoria, it was necessary to hire civilian men and women for training as film handlers for the immense task of viewing, cataloging, and filing the millions of feet of combat film then coming in from all fighting areas.

In order to meet the increasing demand for films of almost every nature in the war effort, hundreds of experts were needed. Thus the Signal Corps complex was staffed by many prominent men from the motion picture industry in Hollywood. It seemed that at one time during the war almost everyone from there was assigned to this former Long Island Paramount Studio. Also many Hollywoodites from the other military film units found reason to make use of the various post facilities.

For some of those permanently assigned it was difficult to make ends meet because the military subsistence allowance didn't take into consideration the high cost of living in the New York City area. It wasn't long before a number of officers, including me, began to see their savings rapidly dissipate. Not that anyone expected to get rich by being in uniform but it would be nice to break even, at least. As frugally as we existed it just didn't work.

Food and quarters, of course, were available to enlisted men. However, some of the well-heeled celebrities lived in posh apartments and frequented expensive restaurants. Several talented creators entered our unit late in the war. Either they enlisted for patriotic reasons or because the draft got hot, or they were drafted and assigned to S.C.P.C. They usually had to settle for low rank, and I was informed that it was not unusual to see some of our buck privates dining at 21 or The Colony with a well-dressed woman or two in tow.

One of the small responsibilities of the Film Library personnel was to burn millions of feet of excess, waste, and dated film. For security reasons, an officer had to accompany two enlisted men and a truck loaded with barrels of film to a designated disposal area once a week. One day the officer in charge forgot to tell the detail not to burn the truck. The post C.O. never let me forget this little aberration.

Later I arranged on my own to have this waste film processed under appropriate security surveillance at the Warner Brothers film salvage plant on Long Island not too far from the center. I had anticipated a favorable reception from the C.O., but for some reason still unknown to me, he refused to take advantage of the opportunity. We continued the burning routine. The salvaging of valuable silver and cellulose base in the nitrate film then in use would have allowed for an appreciable income potential to the government because the Warner's people had agreed to process the film for no charge and credit the Army with the total profits from our material.

I suppose being a subway soldier was better than combat duty, but I took some little comfort in the knowledge that I wouldn't again ask for anything in the Army. Whatever happened was not because of my decisions but those of superior officers. The old Army adage — don't volunteer for anything — struck me quite forcibly after I had been in uniform only a few weeks.

At the time a cousin of mine, Col. Donald Lyon, was in command of the Atlantic Coast Anti-Submarine Air Patrol headquartered in New York City. We were together quite often when I was with the Office of Emergency Management there. Although he had his wife and two children with him, he seemed unhappy to be riding an office desk when his buddies, like Gen. Rosey O'Donnell, were commanding units in combat. Don bugged Gen. Hap Arnold until he relented and told Don to pick up a B-24, fly it via Africa to Kunming, China, and report to General Chenault as his Operations Officer.

Don was elated when I next saw him, and he immediately wanted to get me transferred to the Air Force, and assigned to accompany him to China. I told him not to bother because I was just getting into my job and I didn't know what good I could do for his unit in China anyway.

He was on duty in Kunming only two weeks when, during a Japanese air raid on the distant field, a stray bomb made a direct hit on the slit trench where Don and his staff had taken cover. I was told later by an eyewitness that they were all blown to bits. The military in and out of wartime offers the vicissitudes of many twists of fate.

Military life, at least stateside, is more often boring than tragic. One arranges to get relief from the ennui in some rather insignificant activities, such as the forming of a softball league at the Astoria post. The Film Branch entered a team that Major Richard Maibaum (later an Academy Award-winning writer) dubbed Lyon's Tigers. He headed a team we called Maibaum's Marauders. Capt. Stanley Kramer, the well-known producer-director, was our shortstop, and a good one by the way. Capt. Don Starling, long-time head of film effects at Columbia Studio, was our good pitcher until his glass arm went bad. At least we had some fun and exercise. Bob Benjamin and I received our majorities about the same time so we had the privilege of trading commendations. The extra pay was also welcome.

Because of the limited ratings assigned to our unit it was a continual struggle to get promotions for the men. The extra stripe or two meant recognition and increased pay to those deserving — and most of them were. In our division, those of us in charge of branches vigorously competed for ratings as they became available, but the final decision belonged to Lt. Col. Holman, our Officer In Charge. To this day I know that a few of my men believe they were not promoted because I didn't push hard enough. But that was just another factor of the time that had to be borne in the duties of a neophyte officer.

And to think — the C.O. wanted me to stay on after the war to head the unit. What a dreamer!

At the end of 1945, I was separated from the military and back in civilian life. I had been offered a six-month producer contract with Republic Pictures by Herbert J. Yates, the president. Major Douglas Yates, his son, had arranged a couple of lunch meetings at the New York Athletic Club where the deal was made. This contract was important to me because I had left Hollywood between pictures, so I had no company to return to at the end of the war. Nothing much came of my work at Republic except I had six months to observe the inner intrigues of the studio and get my feet back on the ground, and had a few dollars in the bank for a change.

In due course, I was hired as film editor on *Red River* for producer-director Howard Hawks. The picture starred John Wayne, Montgomery Clift (his first motion picture), Joanne Dru, Walter Brennan, and John Ireland. I went on location in southern Arizona with the company, and a camera unit was assigned to me to shoot cattle drives, spooking cattle, and any second unit production material I could steal when the cast of people and cattle were available. As it turned out I did considerable work, since I was there throughout the six weeks of location shooting.

Because it would be some time before I would be able to start cutting in the studio, I hired a film editor experienced in westerns to assemble the material until I returned. We ran the rushes on location at night and forwarded them to Hollywood so the editor could attempt to keep up with the shooting.

Hawks and the company returned to Hollywood for interiors and I stayed on in Arizona to help Arthur Rosson direct the cattle stampede that was so prominent in the picture. After a couple of days I phoned Howard to see how the editor was making out, and was dismayed to learn that

Howard was most unhappy with the results to date. When I volunteered to return at once to take over and put things right, he suggested I stay on until Rosson had finished and return with him.

Back at the studio, I was summarily dismissed from *Red River* without having seen a foot of the cut film. To this day, I am ever grateful to Howard Hawks for making me available to supervise the editing on *Body and Soul,* because I went straightaway to that assignment and an Academy Award.

When they heard I was free, Walter Thompson and Duncan Mansfield, then cutting for Enterprise Productions, suggested to Lewis Milestone, who was directing *Arch of Triumph,* that he introduce me to Robert Rossen, director of *Body and Soul,* as a prospect for working on the set with him and editing his picture. Rossen immediately had Joe Gilpin, production manager, hire me so I went right to work with Bob in preparation and shooting. It proved to be an enjoyable assignment, working with the director and a cast including John Garfield, Lili Palmer, William Conrad, Joseph Pevney, and Canada Lee.

In order to keep up with the assembling of film during the shooting schedule, I assigned one of my assistants, Robert Parrish, to make a rough-cut while I was occupied with the director on the set. Parrish was pleased to have his first opportunity to make an assembly. Between set-up changes on the stage, I found time to cut some sequences that I saw could be edited for dramatic impact that weren't indicated in the script. It saved time for me to do it rather than to try to explain my ideas to Parrish who, because of his inexperience, was a slow operator.

For instance, I saw a chance to make a transition cut not indicated in the script. One day after viewing the dailies, I asked Parrish to put them aside and said I would cut them when I could get away from the set for an hour or so.

What I saw was a transition beginning with Garfield restlessly sleeping on his dressing room table after a brutal fight with "Ben" (Canada Lee), who died because of it. Suddenly he rose upright, shouting, "Ben!" Rossen had shot the same action with Garfield sitting up in bed in another location that indicated a later time. I believe Rossen and Abe Polansky, the scriptwriter, expected an overlapping film dissolve to indicate a time lapse. Dissolves and black-out fades were the common methods of transition at the time.

I had an idea that a matching direct cut from the start of Garfield's sudden movement to his finishing it in another location would be a startling effect. And it was. I had used it previously with success on an Olivier film in England.

Today most scriptwriters don't bother to indicate time lapse or location movements, leaving it to the director or editor to use what he thinks best. And the best today seems to be the direct cut.

After completion of principal photography, I took over all the reels except the big fight climax that Rossen and Parrish were trying to put together. I needed to recut nine reels to my satisfaction and get them ready for the sound and music editors. In the meantime, Rossen kept after me to take over the end reels because he and Parrish were getting nowhere.

Jerry Young, an able assistant who had worked with me before, had been helping Parrish, and he stayed with me after Parrish left early for another job, with my permission and blessing. On my staff of assistants were Parrish, Young, Jack Gleason, and Mike Luciano, all of whom in due course became film editors. Among assistants on my other films who also became editors, were William B. Murphy, Watson Webb Jr., Russell Lloyd, Peter Bezencenet, Compton Bennett, Richard Van Enger, and Stuart Frye.

Rossen saw little of the results of my work until the preview at the Academy Theatre in Inglewood. Both he and Garfield were overjoyed by the audience reception, with good reason. In all my previews, I have never experienced such an enthusiastic reaction. The relief of witnessing success after months of effort and sometimes anguish was capped when Rossen and Garfield sought me out in front of the crowded lobby and hugged and kissed me to my pleasant embarrassment.

Over considerable resistance from the company executives, I was able to get co-screen credit for Bob Parrish as Film Editor with myself as Supervising Editor. I thought it wouldn't harm me and might help him. Wolfgang Reinhardt, Max Reinhardt's son who was assigned to the picture as the Enterprise representative, didn't believe I should share credit because I alone was responsible for the editing, but he recommended the change because I felt strongly about it. At any rate, *Body and Soul* was voted the 1947 Academy Award for Film Editing, the only one it received, and we will never know if the twists of fate would have deemed it the winner with only my name credited.

It might be of interest to note some of those credited on the picture who later became directors or producer-directors: Robert Aldrich, first assistant director; Abe Polansky, nominated for his fine screenplay; William Conrad and Joseph Pevney, actors; Parrish, and yours truly. Garfield was nominated for his acting performance, one of the three nominations the picture received.

'BODY, SOUL' PACKS WALLOP

Enterprise steps out with a rugged, walloping fight film, exposing the vicious racket still being worked behind the scenes of the boxing game by unscrupulous promoters and greedy managers who allow their boys to fight themselves to death. With newspapers splashing these sordid stories all over its pages, the subject is plenty timely and also boxoffice.

Wisely or otherwise, the original Barney Ross story, which Garfield bought a couple of years ago and out of which this picture stems, was practically thrown out the window. Granted, that a lot of the Ross story would be dated now and perhaps not very conducive to good publicity, but a lot of it was good picture stuff. However, in its place is a hard-hitting and entertaining yarn, with an explosive fight sequence that guarantees to keep any audience on edge.

For Garfield, the part of the money-hungry champ who bets against himself is a cake-walk. He's swell in it. And so is Lilli Palmer, whose quiet, self-assured performance as the sweetheart who sticks by him marks it as her best to date and her as one of Hollywood's contemporary dramatic threats. A great deal of the credit for handling the parts as well as the general lines of the story should go to Robert Rossen, who directed with a sure hand. Participating in that credit should be film editor Francis Lyon, whose expert shearing packs the film with sustained action that makes the rather lengthy 104 minutes hardly noticeable.

Down the cast line the parts, big and small, are well played, with edges going to Anne Revere for her restrained and intelligently sympathetic Jewish mother of the champ, Lloyd Goff for his sharp delineation of the crooked promoter, William Conrad for his down-to-earth description of the champ's manager, Joseph Pevney for a telling characterization as the champ's best friend, Canada Lee for a finely drawn emotional performance as the colored champ who loses both title and life — a sacrifice to the crooked fight mob — and James Burke for his all too brief appearance as his honest and humane, but powerless manager.

Hazel Brooks, hailed as a new find by the studio, rates a separate paragraph, as she does a separate credit line on the film. A sultry, honey-haired blonde, this gal manages an impression in her first screen appearance. Her role as an integral part of the story is relatively unimportant, but as a showcase for her come-hither and otherwise charms as well as her potential talent gets quite a 'play. She is an interesting personality and it will be interesting to watch what she does next.

For Bob Roberts, Garfield's manager, this production is an important as well as a first credit. Technically, the film is a top-grade job throughout. James Wong Howe's photography is of his best, which is good enough. Nathan Juran's art direction and Edward J. Boyle's settings are very creditable, showing faithful reproductions of backgrounds. Original score by Hugo Friedhofer is excellently interpreted by Rudy Polk's direction, as is the title song by Johnny Green, with lyrics by Edward Heyman, Robert Sour and Frank Eyton.

Fight Yarn Gets Rugged Treatment

"BODY AND SOUL"
(Enterprise)

Producer	Bob Roberts
Director	Robert Rossen
Original screenplay	Abraham Polonsky
Photography	James Wong Howe
Musical director	Rudolph Polk
Art director	Nathan Juran
Film editor	Francis Lyon

Cast: John Garfield, Lilli Palmer, Hazel Brooks, Anne Revere, William Conrad, Joseph Pevney, Canada Lee, Lloyd Goff, Art Smith, James Burke, Virginia Gregg, Peter Virgo, Joe Devlin, Shimin Rushkin, Mary Currier, Milton Kibbee, Tim Ryan Artie Dorrell, Cy Ring, Glen Lee, John Indrisano, Dan Toby.

(Running time—104 minutes)

From Hollywood Reporter review.

It is rewarding to be on a successful picture just for the personal satisfaction of believing you have contributed to some degree. To have one's work recognized by one's peers with a nomination and eventual award by the Academy members is most gratifying. Sometimes it opens doors for advancement in other creative areas of production.

But not always. To many it seems to have been the kiss of death. In my case it was some time before any tangible result was evidenced.

REEL 7

JUST WHAT DOES
THE DIRECTOR DO?

My hope had long been to direct but I wished to get a meaningful assignment as my first feature effort. Very few of us independents, however, can afford to be as selective of jobs as we would like because of economic reasons. The decision to accept any suitable spot is obviously influenced by the need of income. As James Thurber said when asked for his formula for success, "Keep on the payroll." To do this, I continued working as a film editor until I could find a good prospect for my directing debut.

It has been well documented that many directors evolved from the film editors' ranks. As examples:

Frank Capra, in his autobiography *The Name above the Title,* described his struggle in his early film career.

Steven Spielberg had experience editing his own films as a teenager, which won him recognition and a chance to direct at Universal, where his first big success was *Jaws.*

Robert Wise edited Orson Welles's *Citizen Kane* among many other successful features before directing a long list of films that include *The Sound of Music* and *West Side Story.* He has served as president of the Academy and the Directors Guild of America. Wise is a good example of the many really fine people in the film industry.

A variety of editing experiences is most helpful to one desiring a directing career in motion pictures. Editing provides an opportunity to study the casts and to understand their diverse personalities and approaches to the job at hand; to learn how directors of divergent abilities handle cast and crew, using tolerance and patience; to discover how to take an intelligent and efficient means to getting proper film coverage in any given environment.

In complete command on the set during production, the director makes his decisions about camera placement, moves, and lens usage. He places and moves his actors according to his interpretation of a given scene. He guides actors in the use of "business" — what they do with their hands, props, and staging on the set, and in the reading of lines. He decides where he wants the camera or actors to move and when he needs close-ups, two-shots, group shots, and long shots.

The resulting film is seen the following day, selection of takes is made, and the "dailies" handed over to the film editor for assembling and cutting.

In any creative endeavor, complete harmony doesn't always prevail. Often the procedure seems to be by trial and error, where anyone's judgment could be considered correct. All things being equal, such as experience and ability, there is considerable chance that conflicts in approach to any given situation in storytelling can be expected. This holds true in the writing, between producer, writer, and director; in the director's interpretation on the set, between producer and/or actors and director; and on through the post-production editing stages.

In the latter stages, for example, an editor and director might quarrel about how the film should be cut, the interpretation of a scene or sequence, or just have a plain old personality clash. Most of the time, however, both are working toward the same end — a good picture. On the surface, at least, they reach a harmonious working arrangement.

At any rate, by guild decree the director has final approval about the cutting of his film until he turns it over to the producer. Fortunately, most often the editing is a team effort with the editor, director, and producer all participating. Within reason, as I have indicated before, the more good minds working in unison on all phases of film-making, the better the result.

Many elements in making a motion picture are subject to frequent alterations. One can't categorically set strict rules of procedure in the entertainment business. Almost every combination of elements has worked, or not worked, according to the attitudes of the time or to some minute differences that alter the precepts just enough to result in quite a different picture. It takes an astute professional to recognize this fact and to compensate for changes in order to make a successful product. That's why they pay those studio heads all that money! Undoubtedly, film-makers will accept a bit of luck with their guessing, too.

Many functions in film-making overlap. For example, the writer confers with the producer in the development of a screenplay. Both consult with the director as soon as he or she is assigned. The director usually works closely with the producer in casting, schedule of shooting, and the final budget.

The film editor enters the picture at the start of principal photography at least, and he too is sometimes consulted about script construction and shooting time. The latter happened on *Red River* when I was assigned as film editor about two weeks before filming started.

The production manager, Walter Mayo, who hired me, asked me to read the script with the thought of suggesting any constructive deletions. There was an obviously repetitious cattle drive river crossing which I brought to the attention of the director, Howard Hawks, at Mayo's prodding. Hawks agreed and told Walter to knock it off the schedule. Later Walter told me that I had saved the company over $50,000. I never saw any of it.

By the way, while on location, Hawks and I drove down to Nogales, Sonora, for dinner one weekend. He told me then that if I ever got to be a director I should never let a production manager influence me about any creative elements. I found out later that it takes some clout to get away with that conviction.

The first Hollywood feature directing opportunity that interested me was a widely read Clarence Budington Kelland story, *House of Cards*. The producers were talking about such stars as Lucille Ball or Ginger Rogers for the lead. I understood that Miss Ball was interested in doing the picture but insisted that her husband, Desi Arnaz, play the male lead. Apparently that wasn't agreeable to the producers and Miss Ball withdrew further consideration.

Miss Rogers asked that her mother be assigned to make some revisions in the screenplay. She worked on it with a clever young writer, Peter Cardoza, for several weeks until the whole project was scrubbed. It couldn't get off the ground for the usual problems of casting and adequate financing, mainly the latter. The picture has not been produced to date, although a film with the same title has been released by Universal.

Fortunately I didn't lack for cutting or supervising editor jobs at the time so I could easily carry on until another chance to direct something worthwhile was offered.

In 1951, the American Cinema Editors, an organization composed of the most experienced and prestigious film editors of the time, was formed. Its purpose is to advance the image and dignity of the film editing profession and to create better understanding among all crafts of picture-making. To that end, for example, the A.C.E. early initiated several successful intra-industry symposiums. Since I was active and concerned for success at its inception, the members elected me president for the first two terms of A.C.E.'s existence.

About the same time, the Film Editors branch of the Academy of Motion Picture Arts and Sciences, of which I was a member, elected me as a representative to the Academy board for two years.

During the two terms of my presidency, A.C.E. held its first symposium, inviting the heads of the creative guilds and unions to gather for a discussion of ways to work together to make better films. At our meeting at the Hollywood Masquers Club, Ronald Reagan, president of the Actors Guild, made a good impression with his presentation. After the meeting he joined a few of us at a nearby pub to evaluate the results, and all agreed that a pleasant atmosphere of cooperation and understanding was created.

At an A.C.E. annual award dinner at the Beverly Hills Hotel, Reagan did a creditable job as Master of Ceremonies. At another dinner George Murphy was toastmaster, Dore Schary (MGM vice president) was the main speaker, and Frank Capra presented the certificates of recognition. Thus, the A.C.E. continued to be a factor in the Hollywood scene.

At a meeting with Charles Boren, secretary of the Producers Association, I suggested that he make a proposal to his board allowing A.C.E. members to use that designation after their screen credits. It was readily granted, and members take pride in displaying their A.C.E. affiliation.

REEL 8

A DIRECTOR AT LAST

In 1952, I accepted an offer to make a TV pilot film in Australia. With a script of an action-adventure story by David Victor and Jackson Gillis under my arm, I arrived in Sydney, not knowing a soul in the country. After about a month of researching and casting, I decided to proceed with the project. After ten weeks I returned with the completed picture for showing. M.C.A.-Revue bought the film, *This is Sydney,* as a one-shot and it has been shown many times on TV. A series could have, and should have, been made.

Francis D. Lyon sets up shots of the Flying Doctor headquarters near Broken Hill in New South Wales, Australia, for Cinerama — South Seas Adventure *in 1958.*

Francis Lyon with crew filming at the Australian Schoolhouse of the Air headquarters where a teacher keeps radio contact with pupils up to 500 miles away.

Most Americans know Australians as a friendly people. I can certainly corroborate that impression because I have many friends there today who made my visits most enjoyable. Subsequently I made two more trips, one to direct the Australian sequences of the successful *Cinerama — South Seas Adventure,* and a business trip in 1959 to discuss terms and conditions relative to organizing and heading a motion picture industry in Australia. Correspondence and conferences with interested Australians went on in Hollywood for several months, but subsequently dissolved because of financial and personality problems in their bailiwick.

A successful film enterprise has now been established in Australia. Costs, terrain, and climate are conducive to efficient production. Crews, performers, writers, and directors are keen and capable, as evidenced by imports such as *Crocodile Dundee*.

An offer to direct a feature film was presented to me in 1953 by Hall Bartlett, a young man who had obtained the rights to use football game film featuring Elroy "Crazylegs" Hirsch, the two-time all-American player at the Universities of Wisconsin and Michigan and all-pro with the Los Angeles Rams. Hall believed Elroy's life had dramatic appeal that would work in a movie.

I surmised that Hall approached me to direct his project because of my editing background, the Oscar, my previous directing experiences, and the fee I would accept. I was impressed with the story he planned to put into a screenplay and with the dramatics of Elroy's life in and out of football. I agreed to direct the film if I approved the script.

The script Hall submitted some weeks later lacked most of the dramatic events he had described, and focused on athletic action. I refused to work with that version and Hall agreed to rewrite it to include some of the more interesting events of Elroy Hirsch's life.

After about three weeks he presented an acceptable work titled *Crazylegs All-American*. We discussed story and script potentials and collaborated to a degree on the final script and casting, with Hirsch portraying himself.

The shooting went fairly smoothly. But one day Hall displayed a trait that concerned me. I hadn't realized just how ambitious he was to be accepted as a producer, writer, and director, even without the experience or background to substantiate these accomplishments so early in his career.

I didn't feel well during a rehearsal one morning. At the lunch break I told the assistant director to call me when the crew was ready for me after lunch because I wanted to rest. The rest lasted longer than I expected with no call. When I went to the set, I was shocked to find Bartlett attempting to direct the scene I had set up before lunch. I stopped this indiscretion and shot the scene my way. I believe he got the message, and I forgot my illness.

Elroy was a natural actor, especially playing himself. He was most cooperative and affable at all times. Lloyd Nolan, Joan Vohs, and the rest of the cast were pros, and the members of the Rams very impressive. Another All-American football player from the University of Southern California, Cotton Warburton, was the film editor, and was nominated for an Oscar for his work on *Crazylegs*. I recommended Cotton to the Disney Studio later, where he stayed for some time.

Being ambitious to direct, I learned that one must be prepared for some reverses of fortune to attain success. There certainly is satisfaction in trying and gratification in accomplishment.

The elements that I believe helped me to be prepared when the long-sought twist of fate offering me a feature directing opportunity finally appeared, would include:

1. My extracurricular activities at UCLA, such as athletics, associations, and my fraternity, Phi Delta Theta, which afforded profitable training in meeting, mixing, competing with, and sometimes speaking before many people of various interests and backgrounds.

2. Mack Sennett's apparent confidence in my ability, shown in his assigning me to direct Bing Crosby in a series of comedies.

3. Self-confidence that developed from experiences in production as an aide to cooperative directors, including Alexander Korda, Gregory Ratoff, Howard Hawks, Arthur Rosson, and Robert Rossen.

4. Responsibilities for solving post-production problems, which included writing, directing, and editing scenes and sequences needed to improve, or salvage, some pictures in Hollywood and England.

5. Robert Kane's confidence in asking me to take over directing *Wings of the Morning,* which I was unable to accept.

6. Several directing jobs on various commercial, informational, and educational films.

7. The Army and governmental responsibilities and irresponsibilities.

8. Winning an Oscar.

9. The Australian TV pilot experiences, *and*

10. Ample opportunity for second guessing directors' decisions and methods as a film editor of major studio and independent productions in many categories and with varied budgets. I had a chance to dissect, study, and reassemble film according to my own judgment to improve pictorial or dramatic effect through techniques not necessarily planned in the script or on the set.

As a wise man said, "When preparation meets opportunity, that's the definition of a break."

Following *Crazylegs,* I took on another sports picture, *The Bob Mathias Story,* produced by William Selwyn and James Fallon, with screenplay by Richard Collins. This was

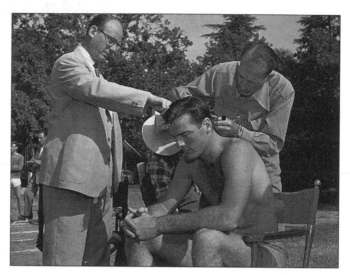

Francis D. Lyon on the set with Bob Mathias while filming The Bob Mathias Story.

a factual presentation of the dramatic events experienced by a two-time Olympic decathlon champion. Mathias and his wife, Melba, appeared as themselves, and Ward Bond played the coach.   Walter Mirisch, an executive with the releasing company, had been resistant to using Melba because he thought I didn't need to be concerned with two amateurs.   I discovered during about three weeks of rehearsals at my home that Melba had natural acting talent. I persuaded Mirisch to let me make a screen test of Bob and Melba to prove my point.   On viewing the test he readily concurred.

The film turned out quite well in spite of being Bob's and Melba's first. Bob later entered politics and was elected to Congress. Perhaps he was well cast in that part, too.

I prize highly a letter of commendation from the famous director, John Ford, whom I had never met, after he had viewed a print of the picture, which Ward Bond had supplied one evening at John Wayne's home. For directing that little Mathias picture of pure Americana, I also received a bronze medallion from Father James Keller and the

JOHN FORD

November 5th, 1956.

Dear Pete:

I had the supreme pleasure and honor of seeing "The Bob Mathias Story" the other night at the home of Duke Wayne...so I must take my pen in hand and write you a fan letter.

Your work, I thought, was really superb. And what performances you got out of those two kids.. Bob and Melba. But who was that horrible sunovabitch who played the Coach? (Incidentally, I am sitting here with Fess and an old character actor named Ward Bond..both of whom send their love.

Again my sincere congratulations,

Jack

J:Fs

Francis Lyons, Esq., 8273 West Norton, Los Angeles, Calif.

Sharing the praise should be the cinematographer, Ellsworth Fredericks; the film editor, Walter Hannemann; and a splendid crew — F.D.L.

Christophers given for "high quality entertainment."

While preparing to direct *Cult of the Cobra* at Universal Studios, I received a phone call from the front office telling me they had just screened a print of *The Bob Mathias Story,* and asking me to help them sign Melba Mathias to a contract. I was pleased at the reaction to her work. But Melba was then pregnant and not interested in a film career.

While I was at Universal, waiting for some script changes I had suggested for *Cult of the Cobra,* Audie Murphy was making his autobiographical picture, *To Hell and Back.* Jesse Hibbs, his director, became ill just before filming final added scenes and retakes, and I was asked to fill in for Jesse, which I was pleased to do.

I found Audie to be a shy, serious gentleman and pleasant to work with. Later on I directed some of his *Whispering Smith* TV episodes.

Through a mutual friend I learned that Audie was a hunting enthusiast. One day I asked him how the deer season was going. He told me those days were over. He couldn't kill anything any more. I guess I showed surprise, because he added that if times were tough, God forbid, and his kids needed food, he would consider a change of heart.

This, after all the medals and acclaim he had attained during World War II for killing more of the enemy than perhaps any other single soldier. Audie Murphy was killed in a private plane crash while searching for film location areas. A sad ending for a real nice guy.

Cult of the Cobra went along smoothly with a good cast and a crew headed by Russell Metty, a very good cinematographer. I enjoyed working with David Janssen, Faith Domergue, Marshall Thompson, Jack Kelly, Richard Long, William Reynolds, Kathleen Hughes, and other capable people in this low-budget film that I've heard the horror-film fan groups have placed on their lists of classics.

Jack Moffitt, a popular columnist on the Hollywood Reporter, surprised me with this complimentary paragraph:

> When a director makes a good picture out of good material, he, of course, deserves a lot of credit. But when a director makes a good picture out of material that most good directors would pass up, he deserves some sort of special award — even though he'll probably never get it. High on the list of such unsung meggers should be the name of Francis "Pete" Lyon. In "The Mathias Story," Pete took three cans of Olympic Games stock shots and two amateurs (Mr. and Mrs. Bob Mathias) and turned out a heart-warming little film whose human appeal and good taste have been warmly commented upon even by the slick magazines, which usually ignore low budget efforts. In "Cult of the Cobra," he has taken the sort of yarn that frequently is seen on Saturday afternoon in a small-town grind house and produced an intelligent horror-suspense story that should advance the careers of everyone in it. A former film cutter, he has but one rule — "Make every character act like someone you might meet in every day life."
>
> —Jack Moffitt

Incidentally, at a meeting while I was serving on the board of the Academy, George Sydney and George Stevens Sr. asked me how many days I took to shoot *The Bob Mathias Story*. At my answer — sixteen — both reacted with surprise and turned away. Somehow I got a feeling there was a bit of incredulity left behind.

This brings to mind a quirk I possessed about ambition. Early in my directing career, talent agents often needled me about my lack of interest in promoting myself socially with influential figures like producers and stars who could be helpful in getting assignments for me to direct more important, big-budget projects. They believed I was able and ready for the "big time," and my socializing more would facilitate their efforts on my behalf. Of course, my success would also be of financial benefit to them with their 10 percent commission because of the higher fees they could ask for my services.

Actually, I was never really concerned about my ability to handle any directing assignment as long as I was able to make the decision of whether to accept it or not. That is why I refused term contracts, which would enslave me to do the company's bidding.

Independence made more sense to me than money, and I have enjoyed the challenges of independence by taking on selected projects that offered such challenges.

I guess I got my "kicks" by beating the odds when they appeared to be against succeeding. A reward in satisfaction of accomplishment, favorable reviews, and comments like Moffitt's article in the *Hollywood Reporter* made it really worthwhile to play it my way.

Directing Walt Disney's *The Great Locomotive Chase* was another challenge offered unexpectedly.

I had heard many favorable reports about the pleasant atmosphere at the Walt Disney Studio, especially from Lyle Wheeler, one of the top art directors in the industry. We had been together at the Selznick studio when I was cutting *Intermezzo* and he was on *Gone with the Wind*. At a time when I happened to be "between assignments," Lyle recommended me to Walt as a prospect for his growing live action program. I have been forever grateful indeed for Lyle's interest.

When Walt first interviewed me I made it clear that I preferred to continue to direct features if at all possible. But he persuaded me (without too much resistance) to help him develop a segment of the *Mickey Mouse Club* TV show he was getting under way. He wanted me to prepare a series of 15-minute segments called *Spin and Marty* from a book by Lawrence E. Watkin titled *Marty Markham*. Larry was then the writer-producer on *The Great Locomotive Chase* at the studio, preparing the script from a book about an actual Civil War incident in which Union spies called Andrews' Raiders tried to run a short train through enemy lines to blow up bridges en route. The survivors were the first recipients of the Congressional Medal of Honor.

Larry's office by chance was next to mine so it was convenient to confer about my treatment of his book for *Spin and Marty* with him and Jackson Gillis, the writer I suggested for the job. The work progressed smoothly. Jack caught on to the spirit of the book, and after we had completed six episodes I took them to Walt for his approval.

At that time Walt was wrapped up in the building of Disneyland in Anaheim. It was a bit of a problem, I thought, because he talked of nothing else from the time I entered his office until I fiddled with the scripts to draw his attention to the reason for my visit.

I already knew about his enthusiasm for the park because he had previously shown me the materials such as the three-quarter-size train cars he was building on the unoccupied stages at the studio. It was a toy of great interest that he loved to talk about.

Finally Walt asked what I wanted to discuss. I told him the production office was pushing to get the scripts in order to make a breakdown for shooting and I wanted to get his approval first. He asked me if I was satisfied that they were ready for that step. I said that I thought they worked and that I wanted to get on to the rest of the thirteen episodes as soon as he approved these.

Walt then told me that if I was satisfied it wasn't necessary to bother him with the scripts and to go ahead with my plans. When I appeared a bit stunned, he said he was too busy with problems at the park and he was sure the project was in good hands. My gut feeling was that he had already read them. Later I learned that Disneyland wasn't his only joy. He had already initiated a plan for a park in Florida. It developed into Disney World and a big success for the company.

The other seven scripts for Spin and Marty went according to plan. Larry was pleased with our progress, and by then he knew very well that I would like to direct his feature. To my great pleasure, he finally persuaded Walt to transfer me to prepare and direct *The Great Locomotive Chase.*

William Beaudine was hired to direct the TV series, and he complimented me for the preparation of thirteen episodes he was presented — a pat on the back I appreciated.

The Great Locomotive Chase starred Fess Parker and Jeffrey Hunter, both cooperative and capable actors and real gentlemen. I also was fortunate to have a very good cast of characters including Jeff York, John Lufton, Eddie Firestone, Claude Jarman Jr., Kenneth Tobey, Slim Pickens, Don Megowan, Harry Carey Jr., George Robotham, Stan Jones (who also wrote songs for the film), and Morgan Woodward. Charles Boyle was the head photographer.

With our wives, Larry Watkin and I arrived in Clayton ahead of the cast, crew, and equipment, to prepare for production by selecting locations as indicated in the shooting script and by searching for local people to fill several parts and add to the atmosphere with their authentic accents and mannerisms. Our success was evidenced by an incident when Ann and I first arrived in our motel quarters. Answering a knock on the door, I was faced by a character who introduced himself as the mayor and said he wanted to welcome us to the town. Upon entering, he pulled a jar from a paper bag and presented it to us, he said, to be sure we were supplied with a local product that the residents were particularly proud of.

He was just the type we wanted to play the part of the rail station yard foreman, and he readily accepted my suggestion that he attend the interview session the next day for a tryout. As a result, he played the part admirably in his scenes, carrying a corncob pipe and showing constant suspicion of the intentions of the main character, James Andrews, played by Fess Parker.

We discovered many capable locals from radio and theater groups and auditions to use as walk-ons. One was Harvey Hester, a prosperous restaurant owner from Smyrna, Georgia, who made a successful impression with his acting ability. (Unfortunately, as often happens in TV versions of theatrical films, a few scenes were deleted, including his. By poor judgment in cuts and trimming, I believe, the picture's entertainment value was damaged to some extent.)

Walt Disney visited us for a few days during shooting and seemed to enjoy the opportunity to get away from

Walt Disney visiting with Ann and Francis Lyon, and alone with Director Lyon on the set of The Great Locomotive Chase *in Georgia, 1955.*

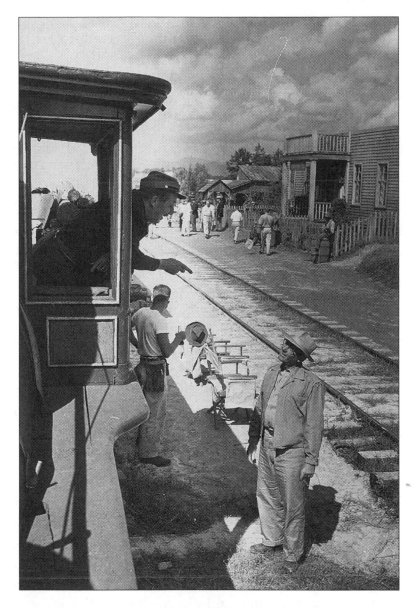

Walt Disney with Francis D. Lyon on location for The Great Locomotive
Chase. *Disney was a train enthusiast. In the background is a station house
for which Peter Ellenshaw painted the second story on glass to be placed in
front of the camera when the scene was shot. This was one of several glass
paintings he supplied to expand production values.*

the studio and spend time around the trains. He never interfered with our efforts in any way.

As a matter of fact, production in Georgia went quite smoothly. Even with a second camera unit shooting process shots for back-projection, which is done at the studio, and the chase problems, including the boxcar wreck, which was a one-shot opportunity, the results were encouraging.

One incident during shooting really shook me up, but only after the fact. The camera crew and I rode a camera-car, equipped with railroad wheels, which we used to shoot a period train engine that was coming at us fairly fast. I started with a closeup of the smoking stack and pulled away to a full shot of the engine coming at us. After the shot, we relaxed and were pleased with it, until Terry Wilson, a stunt man and actor in the film, told me that, although he made his living as a stunt man, he wouldn't do what I just did for any amount of money. When I asked why, he said the engine had no brakes and couldn't have stopped in time if the camera-car had thrown a wheel or broken down for any reason.

No one told me about this detail before shooting. So perhaps it was another twist of fate.

Making the picture was an important experience in my meandering career, and Walt was an inspiration to be around. The studio created an atmosphere of euphoria that I had not previously experienced in any other plant.

By nature Walt Disney was a most affable and warm person to be associated with, in contrast to the sometimes cold, indifferent, and calculating production heads who often seemed more concerned with personal recognition and acclaim than with good movies. Walt was always concerned with the entertainment values and art form of his products and with their effect on others. One never felt that he desired or sought personal glory or the worldwide recognition that he received for his genius.

When working for him, however, one felt compelled to execute his film interpretations rigidly, as evidenced by the ubiquitous storyboards that he had artists draw to his satisfaction for all projects. Eventually, I became concerned that this method of preparation could create a mechanical tone in a film's visual presentation, which would dissipate in some degree the spontaneity directors wish to capture.

Come to think of it, how *does* one explain an attitude so presumptuous as to question any detail of the method used by a man of such great ability as Walt Disney? It came as no surprise when some of my associates and friends questioned my concern that a continuing Disney association might adversely affect my future.

To be thoroughly honest, I was mostly disturbed about the danger of submerging my own initiative, creative urges, and identity entirely under Walt's influence. To do this is to take the path of least resistance and, no doubt, a comfortable life of financial security as long as one would continue to execute Walt's ideas to his satisfaction. But, right or wrong, and whatever its advantages, to submit myself to this kind of life just isn't my nature, which probably could be described as that of a stubborn, nomadic gambler with his own providence. This attitude probably has resulted in many mistakes in judgment in my career, but it has been my life and I've lived it fully.

When we were editing *Locomotive,* Walt indicated that he had nothing scheduled for production in the near future. I had been offered a feature to direct at another studio and, when pressed as to my availability, Walt said I was free to accept it. The Morris office, then my agent, made the deal.

But just before I had finished final editing at Disney's, the Mickey Mouse Club TV Show was released. The *Spin and Marty* segment instantly became a hit, and because of my work on it, Walt asked me to stay on to prepare and direct *The Hardy Boys,* his new TV series.

Walt just couldn't seem to comprehend why I turned down this offer, even when I reminded him that he had willingly allowed me to go and that I was already committed elsewhere. From this experience I soon realized that it wasn't Walt's nature to readily accept or reason with anything contrary to his wishes. In a way it was frightening to be in such a situation, but I must say that when I finally got through to him in detail the reasons I was leaving, he was most gracious and seemingly understanding. He made it clear that he would have come to the same decision. He told me it could get cold outside, but there would always be something for me to do at Disney's whenever I wished to return home. One couldn't ask for more.

Another pat on the back I greatly appreciated is in the letter on the following page. This letter was a surprise coming from a teenager so many years after the picture was released in 1956. In my answer I indicated that I really did enjoy making the picture; that we shot most of it around Clayton, Georgia, a small mountain town near the actual location of the raid and chase; and that the many locals I used for speaking parts and atmosphere performed satisfactory.

October 7, 1958

Dear MR. Lyon:

I am a 16 year old Disney Fan. Unlike some People my age, I really enjoy Disney Films. You directed one of my favorites: "The Great Locomotive Chase." Did you enjoy making the film? Where was it made? I really enjoyed the film. Thank you for using your talents to entertain.

Respectfully,

Jimmie Hollifield II

Jimmie Hollifield II

It is axiomatic, I believe, that creative people in all endeavors thrive on appreciation of their efforts. It is certainly true in the film industry. From my editing days, I recall with pleasure remarks of approval from a director and/or producer when I presented a first cut or made accepted suggestions. For a director, a pat on the back from the producer is a needed ego booster, especially when you're trying to make sense out of a difficult scene or deal with any of the pressures of putting a picture together.

One day, for example, while I was directing an episode of *Laramie* at Universal, John Champion, the producer, came on the set and stopped a rehearsal. What now, I thought? He announced that he had just run the rushes of our previous day's work and they were the best he had yet experienced in the series. There was silence for a few seconds because no one, I am certain, had expected such praise. More often the producer's arrival means an urge to speed up, do retakes or more close-ups, or some other admonishment.

When I caught my breath I thanked Champion and said that if he assigned this crew and cast to me he should always get good results. Ray Renahan, the photographer, was a great help. Needless to say, it was a happy set for the rest of the shooting.

Anticipating critics' or reviewers' comments about your work in the trade papers like the *Hollywood Reporter* and the *Daily Variety* can be nerve-wracking. So much depends upon their opinions, right or wrong, since almost everyone in the business reads these reports. A few bad reviews can hurt, especially one's ego, and favorable ones can get your motor running at top speed. I learned the meaning of euphoria when I got good comments from the critics. Everyone in the field will agree it's manna from heaven.

The following excerpts from prominent critics about *The Great Locomotive Chase* are self-explanatory:

"...Director Francis D. Lyon has kept the chase which occupies the major portion of Walt Disney's "The Great Locomotive Chase" genuinely engrossing. Lyon has rendered this important and difficult element lively and coherent."
The Hollywood Reporter

"...The members of the cast play their roles convincingly under the fine direction of Francis D. Lyon."
The Film Daily

"...Francis D. Lyon, the director, has enacted a peach of a locomotive chase."
Bosley Crowther,
The New York Times

"...Excitingly spun out by Director Francis D. Lyon, "The Great Locomotive Chase" shows heroism and ingenuity."
Rose Pelswick,
New York Journal-American

"...Francis D. Lyon directs skillfully, to get full human values, humorous and otherwise, and really socks it home when the turbulent locomotive chase — a humdinger — gets under way."
Box Office Digest

"...Top credit for the excellence of production and story go to Lawrence Edward Watkin, who wrote and produced, and to Francis D. Lyon for his masterful direction. This looks like a top grosser everywhere."

Showmen's Trade Review

"...Francis D. Lyon has done a fine job of directing Walt Disney's thrilling adventure."
Wanda Hale,
New York Sunday News

"...convincing portrayals are turned in by the cast of "The Great Locomotive Chase" under the able direction of Francis D. Lyon."
Daily Variety

As one might surmise I have albums filled with reviews of shows I have been connected with over the years. I've been lucky that most of them are favorable. But to be fair, I often wonder how anyone not intimately involved in the production of a motion picture can ever know just how and where to assign specific praise or blame for the many facets of excellence or imperfection in the completed product. I feel certain these questions have occurred to many of us while noting the blithe assurance with which newspaper and magazine critics, as well as the self-appointed experts among the viewing public, assign the kudos or deal out the censure for whatever they like or do not like in a picture.

Ideally, the director is perhaps the most important factor in the production of a film, but it would be less than the truth to say that on every picture in this country the director has been permitted to contribute to his ultimate. However, changes in the economics of the film industry in recent years have enhanced the freedom and independence of the director to an extent. Most feature productions today, even those financed by major studios, are in effect independent productions, with only nominal supervision from the financing organization.

This is a contrast from the days when the "major" studios each turned out forty to fifty pictures a year, of which almost all were directed by men under term contract to the studio, making them in effect staff directors. When that was the case, each studio boasted a head of production who often promulgated rigid regulations under which the directors had to work. In at least one studio that comes to mind, the director wasn't permitted to change one word of the script without authorization from the studio head.

Depending upon the relationship between the director and the "boss," or perhaps other reasons, some directors were permitted a degree of influence on the editing of the end product, but for others, their connection with the production was terminated after principal photography ceased.

The status of the director, generally speaking, has improved considerably since the conveyor-belt era has diminished, if not vanished. The Directors Guild of America has contributed to this growing independence. Through the D.G.A.'s efforts, for instance, the director must at least be able to present his "cut" as he wishes after final shooting, though this privilege doesn't preclude the producer from making changes in editing after the director has gone on to another assignment.

The amount and variety of pressure to which most directors are subjected cannot be expressed in a formula that is applicable to all productions. Every project is a story unto itself, and only those closely associated with it can ever say who is really to be praised or blamed for various aspects of the finished picture.

In most cases the director's counsel is sought in the preparation of a final shooting script. But there are isolated instances where he has been advised that he is to handle the material given him, and quite often it is fed to the director after shooting is under way.

It is also usual for a director's advice to be solicited on casting. But on some projects, certain stars suggest or even demand that a producer supply some elements such as cast and even director.

With the star system prevailing, it is not unusual for actors to inject their views into technical matters of production and directing, especially when they are the nominal heads of the producing companies. But even when this is not the case, actors have been known to attempt to mastermind both the producer and the director. Of course, to give due credit, there *have* been instances during the history of the film industry in which the interference, or advice, of a star in matters outside his or her own province have benefitted a production. Again, this contribution is difficult to determine without inside observation.

Few people outside the industry, certainly including some of the critics, have any conception of the tremendous bearing that editing has on the final merit of a picture. I have seen, albeit a very few times, what appears to be an excellent job of writing, directing, or acting virtually ruined by incompetent editing, not always the fault of the film editor because he might have been acting under orders from others. More often, I have seen rather so-so footage transformed into an excellent end product by brilliant editing. Most directors, regardless of technical background, realize that adequate coverage is what makes our pictures flow. Therefore we endeavor to present our producers and editors with plenty of angles to work with in the interest of a good product.

In the final analysis, more often than not you can correctly say "the director did it." But unless you were a part of the (ideally) genuine team effort involved in producing any motion picture, I still say you cannot evaluate with certainty. I honestly doubt, however, that these truths will deter the average critic from assuming he can accurately assess the contributions of the various creators involved in making a particular film.

Ironically, in spite of my resistance to directing television shows for Walt Disney, and my negative attitude in general about working in the medium, it wasn't long before I found myself enmeshed in directing several TV projects. The economic factor was contributory, and principles had to be relegated to the back burner.

While I was preparing a feature that I thought had some potential, I was asked to direct a TV pilot for Twentieth Century-Fox. It so happened that I was stymied by script and casting problems on the feature, so I arranged a leave of absence to do the TV show which, for several reasons, rather appealed to me. Perhaps the fee appealed most. Before the show was finished, Fox offered me a three-year exclusive contract at a surprisingly good salary. I didn't want to tie myself to one studio, so I refused. As it worked out I settled for a nonexclusive pact for six hour-long pictures.

During this same hiatus, I made a quick trip to Lisbon, Portugal, at my own expense, to investigate the feasibility of directing a co-production deal I was offered. The American company expected adequate studio facilities and equipment to be available there as promised by the Portuguese producer. I liked the script they both had apparently approved, and on paper the offer they made me seemed reasonable.

I had a concern, however, that perhaps the necessary elements might not be as promised, and I didn't want to be involved in a project that could be an embarrassing disaster at the start.

My concern was valid because, when Ann and I decided to visit Lisbon, where we had not been before, I was surprised to find very little equipment and few film crew members with know-how available to make a film of the kind required by our script.

We went to Madrid where *El Cid* was shooting because I knew some of the people involved in that picture starring Charlton Heston. One was the production manager, who understood my problem and offered to help by supplying some elements from Spain if I got desperate. But I saw right away that I wasn't going to get desperate. Nothing came of this deal in Portugal, or the feature I was to direct when the script was finished and the casting made final, because of problems with both.

A short time later I was directing some TV shows for Universal. For example, I directed *M-Squad* with Lee Marvin; *Laramie* with John Smith, Robert Fuller, Hoagy Carmichael, and guest stars; *Wells Fargo* with Dale Robertson; *Whispering Smith* with Audie Murphy; and *Kraft Suspense Theatre* with all-star casts.

Speaking of the latter, while I was directing a Kraft show, I had a disagreement with the producer, Robert Blees, who also was the writer, about the opening sequence (the grabber). I wanted to make a stronger effort to get the viewer's attention by creating more suspense than he felt was necessary. Because he wouldn't change the script, I shot it my way and his so we had a choice.

At the time I didn't have a pressing assignment so I was able to work with the film editor and cut it to my satisfaction. I presume Blees approved because it was shown intact.

Fortunately, it received a high Nielsen rating, so high that the studio executives couldn't believe it. Blees asked me to check with my friend Walter Bunker, a vice-president in charge of the Hollywood office of Young and Rubicam, the ad agency handling the sponsor. He certified the report with his New York office. The rating was correct as reported.

This was another lesson that helped me to stand up for my convictions when I felt strongly about them. Of course, good judgment must prevail. One must pick the proper time and place to take a stand and use it effectively.

I must have been in sync with the "twists" because Universal offered me an exclusive directing contract, this time for five years, with options. I was able to resist the temptation and retain my freelancing freedom, which kept me active enough as a director of several television shows as well as a few features.

Some of the other TV series I directed episodes for during the 1950s and 1960s are: *Perry Mason, Bus Stop, Follow the Sun, Adventures in Paradise, Death Valley Days, Man against Crime,* and *Zane Grey Theater.* Features not already mentioned include *Gunsight Ridge* with Joel McCrea, Mark Stevens, and Joan Weldon; *Escort West* with Victor Mature, Elaine Stewart, Faith Domergue, and Rex Ingram; *Young and the Brave* with Rory Calhoun and William Bendix; *Bailout at 43,000* with John Payne, Karen Steele, Paul Kelly, and Eddie Firestone; *The Tomboy and the Champ* with Ben Johnson, Jess Kirkpatrick, Rex Allen, and Candy Moore. Supporting casts included Slim Pickens, Noah Berry Jr., Harry Carey Jr., Ken Curtis, Gloria Talbot, Darlene Fields, Richard Arlen, John Ericson, and Mark Roberts.

The cast from the Perry Mason series. (l. to r.) William Talman, Ray Collins, Barbara Hale, Raymond Burr, Bill Hopper. Francis D. Lyon was the director for a number of episodes.

Director Francis D. Lyon lining up a shot for The Oklahoman, *starring Joel McCrea and Barbara Hale.*

There is more to becoming a director than just getting an assignment. One really doesn't have it made in any motion picture craft until he or she has proven to oneself an ability to fulfill assignments above and beyond the expectations of his or her employers and associates.

Of course, the twists of fate rear their heads here too. If one has the fortunate freedom to select the ingredients necessary to make a successful motion picture, one must consider the choices of story, script, cast, crew, release, budget, and a viewpoint of the subject consistent with the tenor of the time. No matter how much creative freedom he has, a director is ultimately completely dependent upon the audience or, in the case of TV, the advertising buyers, for their receptivity to the subject, stars, and the show's chemistry in general. Those responsible for selecting production elements must be prophetic, talented, damned lucky, or all three, to compile a track record of profitable pictures.

Too often producers or directors are tempted to follow a successful film with imitations or sequels. It appears axiomatic that if one producer has discovered a profitable formula, many others will climb aboard with similar subjects, and a trend is set. It doesn't hold that all those imitations will be successful, because discriminating audiences usually demonstrate that more than just a certain type of show is required to hold their interest. In my opinion, this copycat approach to choosing what films to make has been detrimental, in the long run, to the progress of our industry.

Joel McCrea, Joan Weldon and Francis D. Lyon on location in Arizona for Gunsight Ridge.

REEL 9

WHAT DOES A PRODUCER DO?

In 1966, a new type of market was emerging for feature motion pictures to fill a demand by television stations. Theatrical companies would not supply features to TV, and the television networks were not yet making films of their own. Some associates and I started United Pictures Corporation to produce color feature films aimed principally for the growing syndication and network television markets. I believe we were the first company to enter this field with such a plan.

We produced a program of nine action-adventure pictures with a couple of science-fiction shows included. As the guiding forces of the producing team, Earle Lyon (no relation), a most knowledgeable film-maker, functioned efficiently as executive producer. I had directed some *Wells Fargo* episodes he produced at Universal and thought he fit into our program. Edmund Baumgarten, a former Bank of America motion picture loan officer and former president of Regal Pictures, was in charge of business affairs; I was in charge of production. Fred Jordan, who managed the Producers Studio (now Raleigh), was also a partner. I directed five of the nine pictures we made, and all but the first one, *Castle of Evil,* which was distributed independently, was sold to CBS either for network or syndication.

We believed that a well-mounted product with recognizable names in the cast, made at a modest price, would return a reasonable profit to the production company from the television markets alone. With the foreign markets and local ancillary possibilities such as in-flight,

16mm, and military service, there was substantial potential. This system would work if production and distribution units were in the same company. Television had a voracious appetite for motion picture features and there was an increasing shortage of acceptable products being made for theater showing at the time. A steady flow of suitable subjects for TV seemed marketable.

The network companies had been attempting to supply their own features, which might well have discouraged the independent producers from competing since the networks controlled buying. However, because of overhead charges, the networks and the few major studios able to produce pictures directly for TV use found it difficult to market a suitable product at a profitable cost. We thought they might discover they would have to depend to an increasing degree upon the willing and able independent producers to supply their needs. It was a trend to watch.

In 1965, I realized the need for product on TV when I was at the ill-fated Subscription TV Company in Santa Monica, which had been set up to make films for "pay TV," a short-lived cable TV effort. Network people were often in my office requesting our shows after our use because it was one of their few possible supplies. It was difficult to get suitable products for TV because the major motion picture studios saw television only as competition and were not interested in supporting TV outlets.

However, some elements of the two-market situation have caused producers concern about their future role. For instance, a producer must decide which outlet to pursue in planning his program — films for a theatrical audience or family films more suitable for television. With few exceptions, most films cannot be expected to be profitable in both markets.

Today, the great majority of the movie theater trade is young people under 25. They patronize the sensational subjects and stay away from the "soft" films in droves. So a producer must go the route where he is best suited or can best profit. Either way, it is a gamble.

If he decides to follow the theatrical road he should find satisfying answers to some questions before plunging deeply into that risky market. For instance: how long will the trend to explicit sex, violence, and obscenity be acceptable? How long will the older generation tolerate the exposure of their offspring to this material? What action will censorship bodies and the authorities with power to license movie houses take in face of increasing pressures upon them, such as the protests outside theaters showing *The Last Temptation of Christ?*

Other concerns of a theatrical film producer are: Can a favorable releasing deal be pre-set for the program? Is ample financing available to insure production of a multiple-picture program so the risk is minimized by the law of averages that at least one film will show enough profit to carry the others?

These are difficult questions to answer but the cautious investor certainly wants to be somewhat enlightened. In the meantime, some manufacturers of questionable product forge ahead to their own great profit and, in the opinions of many, to a great loss to the public and the movie industry as a whole. Some believe one can't realistically condemn an industry that supposedly exists to supply entertainment for adjusting to the tastes and choices of the market that supports it.

To those potential audience members who ask, "When are you people going to make films we can take the family to see?," the obvious answer is, "When you evidence a desire for wholesome entertainment by patronizing the theaters that show such films."

Making films for family acceptability, for television, and perhaps for some theatrical exposure, is a tough assignment that requires much creative and production ingenuity. These productions must be budgeted at a cost commensurate with the somewhat limited market of television alone, in the hope of showing a profit down the line. That was the philosophy that United Pictures Corporation decided to follow.

The effort was frustrating at best, because so many elements must be considered in planning, producing, and selling. For instance, will the financing come from a TV network, a very hard nut to crack? If so, one usually works on a step-by-step financial arrangement whereby the TV company supports the purchase of material, then the shooting script, and, when and if it is approved, payment is advanced for production. Usually the TV company must approve story, director, and cast of each project, still retaining right of refusal at completion. A slow, nervous, and cumbersome procedure for an active production company.

The alternative is private financing to make a film on spec. That is, "you make your picture and take your chances" of selling it upon completion. You had best know what the market is and how to satisfy it with a good entertaining product, made with a professional stamp.

After the picture is sold, the TV company that buys it retains the right to edit for its market. It is most frustrating to see one's efforts emasculated by irresponsible personnel for what they claim to be necessary editing for TV, and to insert commercials. After we sweated over lines and scenes for smooth continuity, it was discouraging to have one's efforts denigrated by poor taste, with no recourse available. It would save time and money if such companies would designate guidelines for the producers before delivery so the creators could plan accordingly.

When we organized UPC, with financing by Canadian oil interests, it was our plan to do our own distribution. However, the backers later saw an opportunity to spin off some costs by accepting a distribution deal (and some financing) from Harold Goldman Associates for a healthy percentage of profits. It began to appear that the oil business fell off considerably, but by this time our program was well under way. Our purpose was to present a product that looked much more expensive than its actual cost — professionally produced, well cast, and entertaining, while being made efficiently.

At UPC, we made *Castle of Evil* and *Destination Inner Space* for starters. We used recognizable name actors when possible and paid them well for a few days of work. We hired cooperative cameramen and top technicians who all appreciated the need to save production time.

When I first started directing, I called upon my film editing experience, and decided that using two cameras would sometimes be more expedient than moving one camera twice to get the same coverage. I used this method when I could convince production managers that it would save a day or more of production time.

This two-camera approach saved much shooting time during the schedules we had at UPC. Because of pressure for delivery, I shot principal photography on the first two UPC features, back to back, in 14 days. That is seven days each, for films whose final cuts ran about 85 minutes.

Camera crew and director, Francis D. Lyon, in United Pictures production.
Photograph shows typical two camera use.

I wonder how the Georges Sydney and Stevens reacted to that!

I don't recommend this hurried approach as a practice, because quality has to suffer.

Multi-camera use is common in live TV filming but
not generally accepted in features except on trick action
shots and cases where you may only be able to get one take.
Some directors are leery to use the second camera, no doubt
because they don't know how to place it. One director we
hired to do one of our pictures told me, when I offered him

a second camera, that he had enough trouble with just one camera.

At UPC, we were fortunate to get a couple of imaginative writers. Arthur C. Pierce and Charles Wallace came up with some interesting scripts and were very cooperative in our small production group. Sometimes I wonder if we were a bit ahead of the market at the time.

Other shows we sold CBS include: *Cyborg 2087, Dimension 5, The Destructors, Money Jungle, The Girl Who Knew Too Much, Panic in the City,* and *Tiger by the Tail.* As an example of our casting, in *Tiger by the Tail,* we were able to get Christopher George, Tippi Hedren, Dean Jagger, Alan Hale Jr., Charro, Glenda Farrell, John Dehner, and other competent people. I was credited as producer and Bud Springsteen as director, with Earle Lyon as executive producer.

Of the several knowledgeable production people who saw these films, none came close to guessing the actual costs. For our budgets, we put full value on the screen. One factor that helped was the fine cooperation from the city management and police in Long Beach, California, where most of our city locations were shot.

The cinematographer on most of the pictures was Alan Stensvold, a talented and cooperative technician. He had photographed several of the Bob Hope shows entertaining troops in the theaters of war. Alan was comfortable with the two cameras, and the results were most satisfactory.

I don't intend to prognosticate the destiny of the motion picture business. With all its faults, I still have faith in its continued success. That faith is based primarily upon the upsurge of attention to films of good taste in both theaters and television. But the law of supply and demand prevails. If people want good film entertainment and will pay for it, they will get it. They have the power of protest as to what enters their homes — if they care to exercise it. The future of the film and TV entertainment industry is in the hands of its audience.

REEL 10

FUTURE TWISTS OF FATE

Because of a part-time appointment around 1970 to fill a chair established by the Academy of Motion Pictures Arts and Sciences at the American Film Institute, then headed by George Stevens Jr., I had a new-found interest in the attitudes of the young in their efforts to make it in the movie business. Their aims were various, but primarily toward the entertainment fields. I found the students inquisitive, energetic, and ambitious.

For the most part, the classes were made up of college graduates selected from worldwide applicants who had some experience in film-making at school and evidenced a talent worth developing. A college degree was not a prerequisite, however, because some students were selected on the basis of promising film work in other areas.

All appeared to be keenly interested in the history of Hollywood's growth and the personalities involved. Films of all vintages are screened at the students' request, so they are well acquainted with the stars, past and present.

In a report to the Academy Board of Directors, Frank Daniel, then Dean of Fellows, emphasized how valuable to the education of young film-makers the establishment of the Academy Chair had been for the Institute. He wrote:

> There is no way to overestimate the value of the chair program. Only with this kind of enlarged professional faculty will we be able to truly give all the help that we want to give at the Center for Advanced Film Studies. It was both a pleasure and a

privilege to have someone of Mr. Lyon's professional stature and long experience to help in advising the Fellows. Mr. Lyon was on constant call, giving generously of his time to advise, consult with, and aid the Fellows on their various projects. He not only dealt with editorial problems, from rough cut through finished film, but helped out on preproduction, script analysis and directorial problems. He also participated effectively in our program of screening analysis.

It was while working with one of the Fellows on his film project at the Center for Advanced Film Studies in Beverly Hills that I was asked, "What stars have impressed you most in your motion picture experiences?" For some reason, I had not given much thought to any rating of actors I had contact with during my career. I was actually unprepared to give a realistic response to the question. Offhandedly I stumbled through a couple of names of actors of good talent, but not necessarily impressive. The question created a springboard for some reflection.

I have already noted a few experiences with well-known stars including Laurence Olivier, Charles Laughton, Gertrude Lawrence, Vivien Leigh, and John Garfield. If I define "star" as a leading or recognizable name due to considerable success as an actor or actress in motion pictures, many other names come to mind as thoroughly professional and rewarding coworkers.

As a film editor one has some contact with stars during on-set conferences with the director or at the daily running of rushes. When assigned full-time to the set as a consultant to the director during shooting, the editor has ample opportunity to be associated with the cast in various ways. That opportunity was mine during *Rembrandt* with Alexander Korda, on Robert Rossen's *Body and Soul,* and on Gregory Ratoff's *Adam Had Four Sons* and *Intermezzo.*

On the latter, I recall many pleasant hours working with Leslie Howard and Ingrid Bergman during the staging of their musical numbers. Ratoff didn't like to be concerned with the mechanical problems of film-making, either because of confusion or disinterest, so, to my delight, he gave me the responsibility of directing the principals.

One of the problems in *Intermezzo* was to make Leslie and Ingrid look like the professional musicians they were portraying. It took a trick or two to photograph Leslie in waist-high close shot as he played the violin. Actually there were three men playing the instrument at the same time. One worked the bow with his right hand, and another fingered the strings with his left, both hiding behind Leslie in a tight cramped position. Leslie held the violin with his chin. He timed his moves and facial expressions as the performance of the numbers dictated. With all this trouble, the shots looked very authentic on the screen.

Ingrid was always most cooperative. She practiced many hours learning to finger the keys of the piano in perfect sync to the playbacks. Because of the stars' studied attention to detail, we had no problems in cutting the musical scenes later. The fact that they so graciously accepted me as a substitute director in making a number of intricate shots causes me to place Leslie Howard and Ingrid Bergman on my list of top ten stars with whom I have been most favorably impressed.

There are actors, of course, who have the erroneous impression that the editor can be influenced by extraordinary attention or kindness to favor an actor with close-ups or longer cuts. Of course, the chance of any such influence being effective is minimal.

At the end of shooting of *Intermezzo,* Ingrid Bergman came up to me and said, in that enchanting voice of hers, "Pete, I have a gift for you. Let me get it from my dressing room." She returned a couple of minutes later, holding one hand behind her back. She seemed suddenly quite shy. "Here," she said, thrusting a long, narrow package into my hand. She watched me closely as I unwrapped the gift — a lovely scissors and letter opener set. She gave me a peck on the cheek, and said, "You have to promise not to use those scissors for cutting any of my close-ups!"

Intermezzo was Ingrid Bergman's first American picture. One didn't have to be a seer to know that she would become one of the greats of Hollywood.

It was a pleasure to be with several very impressive actors in Arizona during the exterior shooting of *Red River.* The cast included John Wayne, Montgomery Clift, Joanne Dru, Walter Brennan, and John Ireland, who also represent quite a few Oscars.

Monty Clift was new to films and was very solicitous of knowledge about the medium and of help in his acting — a very serious actor with much talent displayed even at that stage of his career. Clift was an introvert, the opposite personality to Duke Wayne who was always outgoing, but warm and friendly and attentive to his roles. Walter Brennan, a person of great principles and one of the people in the acting profession who was most highly regarded as an actor and a person, certainly is on my top ten list. We had many laughs in the years after that filming, reminiscing about the events in the tent city at Elgin, Arizona, where we were housed.

Later on when he was starring in the TV series *The Real McCoys,* Walter and his gracious wife, Ruth, were invited to dinner at our Hollywood home. It was around his 65th birthday. When they arrived, Walter was in an obviously good mood, and I remarked how well he looked. He said he had just had his annual physical checkup and passed with no problems. He told the doctor that he was often asked how he kept his youthful look and asked if there was an explanation.

"Well," the doctor replied. "Walter, you know I've attended to you for several years and have made many mental and physical tests of your progress. I've determined there is a very simple explanation. You can tell them it's because you have the mind of an eleven-year-old."

I've gotten a lot of mileage with this anecdote over the past years, when I've heard similar remarks about my aging. Someplace along the line, the genes also must have something to do with it.

Another time, Walter told about his early attempts to get acting or even extra jobs at the studios. He and Coop, as Walter called Gary Cooper, used to sit on the curb in front of the Universal Studios casting office, hoping for a call of any kind where they might be used on some director's set.

Walter was a great mimic. One of his subjects was Samuel Goldwyn, the fine producer, who had Walter under contract for some time. There are many Goldwynisms, and Walter was most entertaining in displaying them.

Professionalism in acting is shown in many ways. Henry Fonda was exemplary of the word. Between some television shows I was directing at Four Star, I directed some Rheingold beer commercials with Fonda. He was always on the set ready to be called when needed. He knew

Francis D. Lyon directing Henry Fonda in a commercial.

his lines, was most receptive to direction, and contributed ideas of his own.

Peter Hurd and his paintings were also featured by Rheingold at the time. Too bad President Johnson didn't appreciate Hurd's great talent. After viewing the portrait of him that Hurd had been commissioned to paint, Johnson quickly rejected it as unsuitable for public showing.

Crazylegs gave Elroy Hirsch a chance to show an ability other than as a great athlete. Of course, Lloyd Nolan was the steadying influence on the set — another of the pros who always did a workmanlike job. I recall a pleasant chore at Twentieth Century-Fox directing a *Bus Stop* TV episode with Nolan and Nehemiah Persoff as the leads. What a treat for a director to be blessed with actors of this caliber. Add them to the list.

On *The Oklahoman,* an Allied Artists film I directed, which was produced by Walter Mirsch, I enjoyed working with Joel McCrea and Barbara Hale as the leads. Later I worked with Barbara on a few *Perry Mason* shows. She is always pleasant and a lot of fun on the set.

Speaking of *Perry Mason,* Raymond Burr was one of the really bright actors of our time, in my opinion. Most attentive to his role in a film, he knew his lines perfectly and if he desired word changes in dialogue he always made a point of getting the director's approval before rehearsals. No time was lost in shooting with requests for changes on the set, as I'm afraid happens with some actors. Ray is certainly on my list. Others I have directed or with whom I have had a friendly working association include:

Claude Akins	Howard Duff	Don Megowan
Jack Albertson	Richard Egan	Gary Merrill
Lola Albright	John Ericson	Thomas Mitchell
Robert Alda	Eddie Firestone	George Montgomery
Rex Allen	Christopher George	Audie Murphy
Michael Ansara	Buddy Greco	Sheree North
Noah Beery Jr.	Alan Hale Jr.	Pat O'Malley
Ralph Bellamy	Tippi Hedren	Patricia Owens
William Bendix	John Howard	Leslie Parrish
Ward Bond	Rex Ingram	John Payne
Ernie Borgnine	Dean Jagger	Slim Pickens
Scott Brady	David Janssen	Don Rickles
David Brian	Claude Jarman Jr.	Mike Road
Rory Calhoun	Ben Johnson	Mark Roberts
Rod Cameron	Stan Jones	Dale Robertson
Harry Carey Jr.	Brian Keith	Dick Sargent
Hoagie Carmichael	Jack Kelly	Karen Steele
William Conrad	Nancy Kwan	Mark Stevens
Joan Crawford	Peter Lorre	Marshall Thompson

Ken Curtis	John Lupton	Erich von Stroheim
Linda Darnell	Hugh Marlowe	Jack Warden
John Dehner	Dewey Martin	Joan Weldon
William Demarest	Lee Marvin	Adam West
Faith Domergue	Victor Mature	Jesse White
Ann Doran	Virginia Mayo	Jeff York

At the request of Mike Todd Jr., I directed a screen test for a young man he hoped to use in a feature he planned to produce. To read the feminine part with the boy was Mike's ex-stepmother, Elizabeth Taylor. It would be ridiculous of me not to be impressed with her as a performer. She was very gracious and cooperative that day. I regret not being able to report any other film experience with her.

I find it difficult these days to recall the names of *all* the performers who in the past have made my career a bit more pleasant. To those I have overlooked, my apologies.

Another question I am often asked is: Which of your efforts in editing and directing were the most rewarding? Looking back over so many years, it takes some reflection on the many challenges presented in both categories. I suppose the personal satisfaction comes from the opportunity to contribute somewhat to improvement of the material at hand by ingenuity and imagination.

Of course, I must list *Body and Soul* starring John Garfield as a highlight of my editing career. I was solely responsible for the film's editing and am grateful for its recognition with an Academy Award.

I believe the London Films production of *Rembrandt* starring Charles Laughton was one of my best efforts as an editor. I have seen it on TV after all these years and am impressed with the quality of all elements. It's a pity it isn't in color, and in my opinion it would be a good subject for the new colorization process.

I am well aware of the Directors Guild of America's attitude against arbitrary colorization of films. In some cases, for artistic value, it might be detrimental to the creator's idea of how it should be presented.

Rembrandt was shot in black and white because at that time in England technicolor was just being installed and it was not practical to add the extra time and cost to delay production. This film, with its beautiful sets, is definitely a candidate for colorization. I believe Sir Alexander Korda, the director and producer, would be agreeable to the idea if he were alive.

It seems to me that the producer and director, and the owners, should be the ones to decide on their projects for colorization. An arbitrary rule by Congress or any organization is contrary to a fair judgment, I believe. However, I accept that this is only *my* opinion.

It is possible to overlook many film editing assignments during a career which have not been particularly notable but have contributed to the amalgamation of many successful efforts that have helped make that career worthwhile. I must admit that they all also contribute to the bank account when needed.

One experience that I often think of is working with Eddie Alperson on several low-budget films he made mostly for Twentieth Century-Fox release. He was a friend of the Skouras Brothers, who were at that time influential theater owners. It was always a pleasure to work for Eddie. I recall during a running of one of his pictures to check my editing, he indicated satisfaction with the result, but I saw a few changes that I wanted to make, which I expressed. He turned to me and said, "Pete, don't die from improvement."

I've used that line often since then.

Another time, he called to ask me to edit an upcoming picture. I was about to take some time off and told him I wouldn't have time to take on the job. He said, "Now Pete, you know I want you to do the picture and you can take your time off afterwards. Now, you look in the mirror and you two decide your salary, then go to Oscar (his accountant) and tell him what it is."

I told Oscar what Eddie had said. Oscar replied, "You know why, don't you?" I told him that Eddie seemed to like my work. Oscar said Eddie had noticed that the editing costs on my jobs were by far the least of any of his other films because I finished them in a shorter time. So I made a welcome salary adjustment.

Ancillary incidents sometimes add to unexpected experiences that one remembers years later. Apparently Mr. Alperson told producer cronies about his attitude toward my work. One called, for instance, asking me to look at his picture, which was in the editing stage, because he thought I might help solve some of the problems they were having in putting the film together. He had a good editor, Merrill White, working for him, so I thought the fault must lie elsewhere. At any rate, I was busy and told him that I wasn't able to take the time off. He asked if I could run it at night. Thinking I could discourage him, I said for $500 I would try to fit it into my schedule. To my surprise, he accepted.

As I thought, when I viewed the film, I found it needed help with more than editing. I stayed on with Merrill a few nights to discuss some moves that would help somewhat, but it was a lost cause at best.

Out of left field came a call, when I was "between pictures," from Douglas Fairbanks Jr.'s office asking me to come for a meeting. Doug's problem was a pilot film they had made in Mexico on which the sound was not of commercial quality. Since I was available, he asked me to go to Mexico City to see if it could be corrected. Not my major area, but I decided to take Ann along and see what could be done.

Their technicians were very cooperative and efficient, and I quickly found the trouble. We redubbed the sound track with good results. I don't know what became of that film, but I enjoyed the experience and appreciated the confidence Douglas had in me to do the job.

For satisfaction in directing, I would include *The Bob Mathias Story,* which received very good reviews and the Christopher Award. My pre-production, casting, directing, and post-production contributions were indeed rewarding.

The Walt Disney film, *The Great Locomotive Chase,* was an important assignment for me and must be mentioned as an accomplishment of great satisfaction.

We can't overlook the outstanding creative contributions film writers have made to the success of our industry. "If it ain't on paper, you ain't got it" certainly applies to making movies.

Producers understandably bid for film rights to best-selling books because the stories have already been well received. It's like having a successful preview even before a film is made.

Of course, sources of acceptable stories for films are varied. Newsworthy events, history, biographies, magazine articles, original ideas, and many other possibilities are available.

For movies to be produced, the writer is normally the first to be assigned. With the producer, and sometimes the director if he is already committed, a plan is discussed for treatment with the writer, who then puts it in screenplay form.

A successful screenplay writer knows the mechanics of film-making and what is desired to get all the dramatic values on paper. He designates his ideas for camera set-ups, the movements and "business" of casts, time lapses, transition, and the like, in the completed script as a guide for the director, who may not always follow script directions. He might rely upon his own interpretation of the action. Usually, however, there is agreement on the approach to follow.

Some writer-director teams have been outstandingly successful. Frank Capra and Robert Riskin, for instance, worked together on *It Happened One Night,* an original story by Arthur Caesar that was adapted to the screen by Riskin. The earlier team of Ben Hecht and Charles MacArthur wrote the original story *The Scoundrel* among other good movies of the time. Both films were Oscar winners.

Some names of outstanding screenwriters that come to mind are Nunnally Johnson, George Seaton, Dudley Nichols, Budd Schulberg, Charles Brackett, Frances Marion, Daniel Taradash, and Alan Jay Lerner. But why get into names? There are so many talented writers who deserve mention.

Many films credit several writers. They include categories for "original story," "adaptation by," "screenplay by," "original story and screenplay by," and so on. Sometimes several writers are assigned to re-write what others have attempted. As they say, scripts are not written, they are rewritten.

When I am asked by aspiring students how they can get into the movie business, I often suggest that if they think they have the talent they should try to write their way because there always is a market for good stories. They can even try to write for their favorite TV shows if they believe they can do as well as the people currently writing the scripts. At any rate, it isn't easy, but the twists of fate could make it worthwhile.

In summation, the *producer* is generally the one who puts together the elements that make a movie. They include finances (a necessity), the story, the writer, director, the cast, the film editor, the crew, and the producer's supervision of all.

The *writer* puts it on paper for all to make judgment.

The *director* transfers what is on paper to live action on film.

The *film editor* puts the film together to make the completed project for theater showing.

It is most gratifying to have been associated all these years with so many dedicated persons in the movie business, both in front of and behind the camera. As time progresses, their ranks will be filled to a large degree by the many bright students of film who are seizing opportunities today to develop their talents on a scale never before dreamed of. The recognition and acceptance of their abilities should contribute impressively to a noticeable advancement in the quality of films for all purposes.

However, the industry will have to struggle along somehow without my help in the future, because I am happily retired and no longer plan to be active in production. I intend to follow it, however, with considerable interest since the business has been so good to me for many years.

I shall be ever thankful for those twists of fate that have guided me to and during this unfading, unforgettable career, and I shall always appreciate the opportunities they have afforded me to contribute in some way to the development of an exciting enterprise.

To all those who follow —

May the Twists of Fate be favorable!

EPILOGUE

The following appeared in the Bowbells, North Dakota, newspaper:

Dear Editor:

I am a lover of movies and theatre and need your help as follows.

I wish to contact the well-known movie director (and editor) Francis D. "Pete" Lyon, who was born at Bowbells on July 29, 1905, but I don't know how to trace him, also because I am not sure that he is still alive. On the contrary, I think he may be deceased since I don't see his name and address in a very recent American Movie Directors' Directory.

In any case, if he were deceased, I should be equally pleased to locate his immediate family and then ask you to seek in the files of this town hall if any heirs or relatives of his are available in the Bowbells whereabouts.

If you can locate somebody, please send me name and address of at least one of these persons who, surely, will be able to indicate to me if the director Lyon is still alive and his address or the address of his immediate family, if he were deceased.

Roberto Recanatesi

Ancona Italy

The newspaper put me in touch with the letter writer. After I corresponded with him, I received the following letter:

Ancona, Italy

December 4, 1985

Dear Mr. Francis D. Lyon,

I thank you very much for your kind letter and photo and also want to thank that kind lady from Dakota who had forwarded you my inquiry.

You have well guessed. I am a young Italian fan of yours and lover of theatre and cinema (very much of the American ones). May I say, without conceit, I am quite knowledgeable about them (particularly the ones of the far-off years ... it's curious).

I am starting a career as an actor (an old dream of mine). I recently graduated as a lawyer, too, but I must confess this career has no real appeal for me. My heart lies in the theatre.

I have a large private collection of screen and stage memorabilia all over the

world and have wished to have a photo
with dedication from you for my important archive, which I am preparing with
real passion and tenaciousness and which
I plan to pass on to any important and
interested Italian institution.

Several famous American directors
already answered me with photos. I usually write to them via the Directors Guild
of America, Inc. Since I have read that you
have been by now outscreen (is it true?) at
least as a director, I was not sure they
could have a forwarding address for you.
(They, for instance, have no forwarding
address for Mervyn Le Roy or Hugo
Fregonese or the younger John Milius, etc.
Can it happen that a famous American
director is not a member of this important
guild?) And then I thought it right to write
to the City Clerk of your native city.

Sometimes I make use of this system,
when I wish to trace a retired artist whom
I am interested with. I have recently done
the same also with the 1930s movie star
Jean Parker, who is unknown at every
Hollywood union or movie institute. Even
the well-furnished *Christensen's Ultimate
Movie, TV and Rock Directory* (Cardiff-by-
the-Sea publications) has no forwarding
address for her.

Your biography here in Italy is reported only in the *Filmlexicon* (1970 or
1971), and I may read on it the titles of

many films of yours (either as an editor or as a director) which I saw and appreciated.

I much enjoyed the British films you were editor of: *Things to Come* (1936 — co-editor was Charles Crichton, later a renowned director too), *Rembrandt* (1937), *Knight without Armour* (1937) with Dietrich; *Intermezzo* (1938), and *Day-Time Wife* (1939) both by Ratoff; as well as some American ones, *I Was an Adventuress* (1940), *The Great Profile* (1940), *Adam Had Four Sons* (1941), *Body and Soul* (1947, by Rossen, Academy Award for you), *Ruthless* (1948), *Dakota Lil* (1950), *The Sword of Monte Cristo* (1950), *He Ran All the Way* (1951), and your last excellent proof as an editor, *The Diamond Queen* (1953).

As to your films as a director, I see with much pleasure that you were very versatile and, above all, admirable in directing the actors and reconstructing environments and atmospheres. I see that you are remarkable either in the horror or thrilling kind or in the western or sporting kind. Perhaps your films are not particularly famous. However, I see that you often called famous actors to star in them, and some of them are really curious and interesting. For instance, *The Great Locomotive Chase* (1956), *Destination Inner Space* (1966), *Castle of Evil* (1954), *Crazylegs* (1953), and *The Bob Mathias Story* (1954), curious biography of a Yankee champion.

I enjoyed also: *The Cult of the Cobra* (1955), *Bailout at 43,000* (1957), *The Oklahoman* (1957), *Gunsight Ridge* (1957), *Escort West* (1958), *The Young and the Brave* (1963), *The Girl Who Knew Too Much* (1968), and *Tiger by the Tail* (1970) by R.G. Springsteen, which you were only producer of. However, other films of yours as editor or director are unknown in Italy.

Please accept my warmest thanks, greetings, and apologies, for this trouble, and warmest esteem always! Best wishes to your life and thanks again for the photo.

Yours truly,
Roberto Recanatesi

INDEX

Page numbers in italics indicate a photograph or other illustration. Capital letters in parentheses following film titles show the following involvement of Francis D. Lyon:

> (CD): co-director
> (D): director
> (E): editor
> (P): producer
> (SE):supervising editor
> (W): writer

The Girl Who Knew Too Much, 199, 221
Money Jungle, 199
Panic in the City, 199
Tiger by the Tail, 199, 221
Lyon, Sumner, 137
Lyon, William, 139

MacArthur, Charles, 214
McCrea, Joel, 187, 209
McCroskey, H. E., 19
Maibaum, Richard, 144
Man Against Crime (D), 187
Man Who Could Work Miracles, The, 65, 69, 70, 71
Mann, Ned, 69, 75, 77-78, 85
Marion, Frances, 214
Marquette, Desmond, 136
Marvin, Lee, 186
Mary Poppins, 87
Mathews, Dave, 137
Mathias, Bob, 165-168, 169, *166*
Mathias, Melba, 166, 168, 169
Mature, Victor, 187
Mayo, Archie, 121
Mayo, Walter, 155-156
Men in Her Life, The (E), 21
Menjou, Adolph, 28
Metty, Russell, 168
Mickey Mouse Club TV Show, 171, 178
Mirisch, Walter, 208
Mock, Jane and John, 75
Moffitt, Jack:
    and column in *Hollywood Reporter,* 169, 170
Money Jungle (D), 199
Moore, Candy, 187
Moscow Nights (E), 59, 60, 65, *66,* 67 (titled *I Stand Condemned* in U.S.A.)
Moviola, 27-28, *27*
M-Squad (D), 186
Munich crisis, 110
Murphy, Audie, 168, 186
Murphy, George, 157

Mussolini, 105, *106,* 107
    and decorating Rome for Hitler's arrival, *104*
My Fair Lady, 92
Negro Colleges at War (P/D/W), 125
Nichols, Dudley, 214
Nolan, Lloyd, 164, 208

Oberon, Merle, 53
Odd Man Out, 2
Office of Emergency Management (O.E.M.), 124
Office of War Information (O.W.I.), 124
Ogilvie, Jack, 139
Oklahoman, The (D), *188,* 208-209, 221
Old Ironsides, 17
Olivier, Laurence, 59-60, 92, 204
Orlebeck, Les, 136
Oscar, vii, 3

Palmer, Lili, 146
Panic in the City, 199
Parker, Fess, 173
Parrish, Robert, 1, 2, 146, 147, 148
Pascal, Gabriel, 101, 102
Payne, John, 187
Pearl Harbor, 123
Perry Mason (D), *187,* 209
Persoff, Nehemiah, 208
Pevney, Joseph, 146, 148
Pharmacist, The, 47
Phi Delta Theta International Fraternity, 16, 21, 164
Picture of Dorian Gray, The, 92
Pierce, Arthur C., 199
Pinewood Studios, 97
Polansky, Abe, 148
Prelude to War, 139
Previewing, values of, 38
Private Life of Don Juan, The, 64
Producer, duties and responsibilities of, 193-200, 215

PHOTOGRAPHS AND ILLUSTRATIONS